The Year of the Poet XI

April 2024

The Poetry Posse

inner child press, ltd.

The Poetry Posse 2024

Gail Weston Shazor
Shareef Abdur Rasheed
Teresa E. Gallion
hülya n. yılmaz
Noreen Snyder
Tzemin Ition Tsai
Elizabeth Esguerra Castillo
Jackie Davis Allen
Mutawaf Shaheed
Caroline 'Ceri' Nazareno
Ashok K. Bhargava
Alicja Maria Kuberska
Swapna Behera
Albert 'Infinite' Carrasco
Michelle Joan Barulich
Eliza Segiet
William S. Peters, Sr.

In order to maintain each poet's authentic voice, this volume has not undergone the scrutiny of editing. Please take time to indulge each contributor for their own creativity and aspirations to convey their uniqueness.

hülya n. yılmaz, Ph.D.
Director of Editing ~
Inner Child Press International

General Information

The Year of the Poet XI
April 2024 Edition

The Poetry Posse

1st Edition : 2024

This Publishing is protected under Copyright Law as a "Collection". All rights for all submissions are retained by the Individual Author and or Artist. No part of this Publishing may be Reproduced, Transferred in any manner without the prior **WRITTEN CONSENT** of the "Material Owners" or its Representative Inner Child Press. Any such violation infringes upon the Creative and Intellectual Property of the Owner pursuant to International and Federal Copyright Laws. Any queries pertaining to this "Collection" should be addressed to Publisher of Record.

Publisher Information
1st Edition : Inner Child Press
intouch@innerchildpress.com
www.innerchildpress.com

Copyright © 2024 : The Poetry Posse

ISBN-13 : 978-1-961498-24-2 (inner child press, ltd.)

$ 12.99

WHAT WOULD
LIFE
BE WITHOUT
A LITTLE
POETRY?

Dedication

This Book is dedicated to

Humanity, Peace & Poetry

the Power of the Pen

can effectuate change!

&

The Poetry Posse

past, present & future,

our Patrons and Readers &

the Spirit of our Everlasting Muse

*In the darkness of my life
I heard the music
I danced…
and the Light appeared
and I dance*

Janet P. Caldwell

Table of Contents

Foreword	*ix*
Preface	*xiii*
Renowned Poets	*xv*
William Butler Yates	

The Poetry Posse

Gail Weston Shazor	1
Alicja Maria Kuberska	9
Jackie Davis Allen	15
Tezmin Ition Tsai	21
Shareef Abdur – Rasheed	27
Noreen Snyder	35
Elizabeth Esguerra Castillo	41
Mutawaf Shaheed	47
hülya n. yılmaz	55
Teresa E. Gallion	61
Ashok K. Bhargava	67
Caroline Nazareno-Gabis	75

Table of Contents ... *continued*

Swapna Behera	81
Albert Carassco	87
Michelle Joan Barulich	93
Eliza Segiet	99
William S. Peters, Sr.	105

April's Featured Poets — 111

Hassanal Abdullah	113
Johny Takkedasila	119
Rajashree Mohapatra	127
Shirley Smothers	133

Inner Child Press News — 139

Other Anthological Works — 179

Foreword

Renowned Poets

William Butler Yates

Each month, the Year of the Poet features a themed poem, and it gives me pleasure to invite readers to peruse the poems in this, the April 2024 issue.

Members, by name, The Poetry Posse, are invited to submit three poems, the first being a poem inspired, this month by the poet, William Butler Yates. We each, also submit two additional poems each month. These poems may or may not be inspired by the current issue's theme, whether penned in the poet's style or not. Or simply inspired by researching more about personal life of William Butler Yates.

Be assured that there is a wealth of poetry awaiting your perusal in this month's Year of the Poet.

Elsewhere, in this magazine, you will find an Introduction providing more and pertinent information about the Irish poet, Yates. I encourage you to avail yourself of that information.

Further research will provide you with his poetry, that, to this day, inspires other poets. Yates, encouraged younger poets, for instance, Ezra Pound.

As a child, I remember hearing that my ancestors hailed from Ireland. As yet, that is not proven. At least to my knowledge. Nevertheless, living in southwestern Virginia, confined in Appalachia, by the Cumberland Mountains and snaking roads, no sidewalks, the sun arriving only at noontime, the moon, the size of a skinny, slivery slip of pale ivory, I longed for that which was not within my reach.

And poetry, to some extent, satisfied that need. It has taken me, then, as a child to places that my mind had never known! And, it still does!

I applaud you, the readers who hold this book in your hands. As you read, may you discover more about the poet William Butler Yates. And as you do, may you, possibly, discover something about yourself from the additional poetry contributions of The Poetry Posse! Could it be that there is a poetic voice within you, calling out, awaiting invitation to express itself?

Jackie Davis Allen
Poet, Artist
Northern Virginia

Now Available

www.innerchildpress.com/world-healing-world-peace-poetry

Coming May 2024

www.innerchildpress.com/now-open-4-submission

Preface

We, **Inner Child Press International, The Year of the Poet** and **The Poetry Posse** welcome you.

WOW . . . a decade +. We continue to be excited as we have now crossed over into our 11th year of **The Year of the Poet**.

This particular year we have chosen to feature renowned poets of history. We do hope you enjoy. Read ~ Learn.

For those of you who are not familiar with our story, back in 2013, a few of us poets got together with the simple intention of producing a book a month. That was our challenge. Since that time the enterprise has blossomed and brought forth a fruit that seems to keep on growing as evidenced as we enter 2023.

Our purpose is simple. Through our lyrical words and verse, we not only wish to share our poetic works, but we also have the poetic naiveté to believe that we can assist in the growth of consciousness of the things that have an effect our collective humanity. Therefore, we welcome your readership. For more about what we are attempting to accomplish, have a look at our Publishing Web Site . . . www.innerchildpress.com. If you would like to know a bit more about this particular endeavor please stop by for a visit at :

www.innerchildpress.com/the-year-of-the-poet

Over the years, Inner Child Press has been socially active to bring awareness and catalog through literature the things that have an impact upon our world and its inhabitants. We have solicited, produced, underwritten and published quite a few volumes to that end. For more insight you may wish to visit : www.innerchildpress.com/the-anthology-market. If you are a writer, poet, or activist, you would be advised to keep a eye out for upcoming volumes should you desire to participate. All readers are welcomed as well. Note, that there is a myriad of published volumes that are available as a FREE PDF download as well as available for purchase at affordable prices.

We at this time extend to you our well wishes for your own personal journey and hope that you consider including us as a travel companion.

Bless Up

Bill

William S. Peters, Sr.

Publisher
Inner Child Press International
www.innerchildpress.com

Renowned Poets
William Butler Yeats
1865 ~ 1939

April 2024

by hülya n. yılmaz, Ph.D.

The Nobel Prize laureate Dubliner poet and playwright was born to a father, who was a lawyer and a prominent portrait painter, and a mother, who was the daughter of a successful merchant in Sligo, in western Ireland. He completed his education in Dublin and London and was involved in the Londoner *fin de siècle*. The young Yeats actively participated in and contributed to societies that were committed to revive Irish literature—known as The Irish Dramatic Movement. In collaboration with Isabella Augusta, Lady Gregory, a dramatist and folklorist, he founded the Irish Literary Theatre, aka the Abbey Theatre and served as its chief playwright. Yeats dedicated the early period of his life to composing plays, on Irish legends for the most part.

The *Dublin University Review* was the first to introduce Yeats to the public in 1885 by releasing his two poems, "Song of the Fairies" and "Voices", and an essay, "The Poetry of Sir Samuel Ferguson". In 1886, his "Mosada" was printed privately by the same publisher as a booklet that appeared in the form of a short verse play. His first poetry collection which reflects his fascination with Irish sagas, mysticism and spiritualism was published in 1887. Scholars of the field assert that Yeats began a claim to fame following the publication of "The Wanderings of Oisin" and his other poems in 1889. Venturing into a path beyond the frequently-traveled one, we shall now use a little poetic license to allow a voice to our own views:

> We who are old, old and gay,
> O so old!
> Thousands of years, thousands of years,
> If all were told:
> Give to these children, new from the world,
> Silence and love;
> And the long dew-dropping hours of the night,
> And the stars above:

> Give to these children, new from the world,
> Rest far from men.
> Is anything better, anything better?
> Tell us it then:
> Us who are old, old and gay,
> O so old!
> Thousands of years, thousands of years,
> If all were told.

"If all were told: / Give to these children, new from the world, / Silence and love [. . .]" William Butler Yeats observes, and raises a timeless question: "Is anything better, anything better?" A question worth our contemplation, is it not?

hülya n. yılmaz, Ph.D.

Professor Emerita (Liberal Arts),
Penn State, U.S.A.
Director of Editing Services at
Inner Child Press International, U.S.A.

*Poets . . .
sowing seeds in the
Conscious Garden of Life,
that those who have yet to come
may enjoy the Flowers.*

Poets, Writers . . . know that we are the enchanting magicians that nourishes the seeds of dreams and thoughts . . . it is our words that entice the hearts and minds of others to believe there is something grand about the possibilities that life has to offer and our words tease it forth into action . . . for you are the Poet, the Writer to whom the Gift of Words has been entrusted . . .

~ wsp

Poetry succeeds where instruction fails.

~ wsp

Now Available

www.innerchildpress.com/the-anthology-market.com

Gail Weston Shazor

Gail Weston Shazor

Gail Weston Shazor is a lover of words. She is fond of the arcane, unusual and the not yet words.

Coining words at an early age, there was often a bit of trouble with teachers, but she always had her mother and aunt to back up her choices in expression. Born in Mississippi, she spent her early years with her grandparents. Each of the four left very careful influences on her pre-schooling. She learned in turn how women worked in and out of the home and how men worked in and out of the home to support the family. She learned that a lack of proper schooling was not the only way to learn and understanding life was a great teacher. As in most rural families of color, women had a greater chance of formal learning. Both of Gail's grandmothers read out loud to the family whether it was the bible or the newspapers and important documents to their spouses.

Gail Weston Shazor has authored (so far) Notes from the Blue Roof, A Overstanding of an Imperfect Love, HeartSongs and Lies My Grandfather's Told Me. The number of anthologies is too many to list with the premier accomplishment of one of the contributors to The Year of The Poet. Gail will always lend her ink to community projects and will purchase the books of fellow poets in the Inner Child Press family.

Fae

I would steal
Your joy
Your laughter
Your smiles
Your years
For I know not
Tears in rain
Eyes closed against the sun
Sorrow at death
I may scare you
Sometimes
Because I want
What you have
and have always desired
Humanity

Neon Noise

Bottle ringing
Ringing singing
Turned on their side
With the hole
In the bottom
Prescient
Waiting lingering
To be served
With a forefinger and thumb
Ready
Glinting glasses
Clinking toasting
Amber blurs
On the muzak
Long Miles to go
Blues in bitter fruit
Salty sweet
Stretching post to post
Markers
In unlit cigars
Clenched between teeth
Screaming
I can't hear
You

Listen, Listen

Y'all better listen quick
Somebody trying to learn
You something
It ain't when they got you
That you in trouble
Cause another man done gone
From the county farm
The gate was left just a bit ajar
Just a bit so he could see
And the others said
Nah man
This is protective custody
In here we safe
And they waited for the feeding time
Stuff slid under the door
Thrown over the fence
To keep everyone from roaring
The only bit of lightness
Was the complexion of the hand
They had been trained not to bite
But the door called out
Swinging gently on its rusty hinge
Singing slyly and waiting
Freedom oh freedom
Was its plaintive plea
And he knew the sun actually shone
Beyond this protection
Because he had been there
Free
From the county farm
The chains had been left long enough
Just so he could walk, text and surf

The Year of the Poet XI ~ April 2024

Gone were the days of hoops
And playgrounds on the corner
Time spent listening to learned ones
Listen, Listen
There is no razor wire up top
And he gave himself away
Until no one knew who he was
They didn't know his name
In the factories built on paddies
Just another Joe

The tables had been turned on
Turntables
From which prophets speak
Was that the music
Or just the others
Nah man
This is where it's at
And they turn the volume up louder
Another man done gone
Another man done gone
Awaken to the message
Of the leaders voices but it
Ain't you
Because you too scared of the song
The gate is whispering to you
Third eye close to the call
Of the drumbeat
And you won't be the man
That they kill
For running away
Because they got you tracked
GPS
Smartphones

Gail Weston Shazor

Chips in everything you bought
Listen, Listen
Another man done gone
I didn't know his name
He had broken the long chain
Slipped through the gate
Found out who he was
And tried to save you
But you chose to stay in protective custody
They killed another man
Another brother done gone
Into the network.

Alicja Maria Kuberska

Alicja Maria Kuberska

Alicja Maria Kuberska – awarded Polish poetess, novelist, journalist, editor.

She is a member of the Polish Writers Associations in Warsaw, Poland and IWA Bogdani, Albania. She is also a member of directors' board of Soflay Literature Foundation, Our Poetry Archive (India) and Cultural Ambassador for Poland (Inner Child Press, USA)

Her poems have been published in numerous anthologies and magazines in : Poland, Czech Republic, Slovakia, Hungary,Ukraina, Belgium, Bulgaria, Albania, Spain, the UK, Italy, the USA, Canada, the UK, Argentina, Chile, Peru, Israel, Turkey, India, Uzbekistan, South Korea, Taiwan, China, Australia, South Africa, Zambia, Nigeria

She received two medals - the Nosside UNESCO Competition in Italy (2015) and European Academy of Science Arts and Letters in France (2017). Ahe also received a reward of international literary competition in Italy „ Tra le parole e 'elfinito" (2018). She was announced a poet of the 2017 year by Soflay Literature Foundation (2018).She also received : Bolesław Prus Prize Poland (2019), Culture Animator Poland (2019) and first prize Premio Internazionale di Poesia Poseidonia- Paestrum Italy (2019).

William Butler Yeats

Celtic Songs

Ireland can't be
defined in a few lines,
closed within a picture.

It is hard to find old spells
- elusive, forgotten words.
It is not easy to describe with a pen
wind whistling ancient sagas,
resurrect dead heroes,
revive cut down, sacred trees.

Shadows of the druids,
similar to huge oak trees,
emerge from the twilight.

Their roots grow deeper and deeper
in people's hearts and minds
to leave a trace in the words of the songs
- they never forget to hum
about pride, courage, freedom.

On the Bench

A hunched old woman,
with a face like an autumn leaf,
sat down in front of the house.

The sun and wind carved
deep wrinkles on her face,
the blue veins wrapped
around her tired hands.

Nothing is happening today.
She doesn't remember
what happened yesterday
- the past returns like waves.

A girl is sitting on a bench.
biting unripe apples
stolen from a neighbor's orchard.

Alicja Maria Kuberska

Time Differences

We walk past each other
and we say casual greetings.
You won't catch up with me.
Merciless clocks mix
my days with your nights.

We agreed not to meet.
We pass one another
like the sun and the moon.
We touch each other with words
to leave in a moment.

Picasso paints in our imagination.
He brightens our dark planes,
adds color to grays,
sketches in unexpected curves.

Jackie Davis Allen

Jackie Davis Allen

Jackie Davis Allen, otherwise known as Jacqueline D. Allen or Jackie Allen, grew up in the Cumberland Mountains of Appalachia. As the next eldest daughter of a coal miner father and a stay at home mother, she was the first in her family to attend and graduate from college. Her siblings, in their own right, are accomplished, though she is the only one, to date, that has discovered the gift of writing.

Graduating from Radford University, with a Bachelor's of Science degree in Early Education, she taught in both public and private schools. For over a decade she taught private art classes to children both in her home and at a local Art and Framing Shop where she also sold her original soft sculptured Victorian dolls and original christening gowns.

She resides in northern Virginia with her husband, taking much needed get-aways to their mountain home near the Blue Ridge Mountains, a place that evokes memories of days spent growing up in the Appalachian Mountains.

A lover of hats, she has worn many. Following marriage to her college sweetheart, and as wife, mother, grandmother, teacher, tutor, artist, writer, poet and crafter, she is a lover of art and antiques, surrounding herself, always, with books, seeking to learn more.

In 2015 she authored *Looking for Rainbows, Poetry, Prose and Art*, and in 2017, *Dark Side of the Moon*. Both books of mostly narrative poetry were published by Inner Child Press and were edited by hulya n. yilmaz in 2019, *No Illusions. Through the Looking Glass*, which was nominated to be considered for a Pulitzer Prize by the publisher and editor of Inner Child Press, ltd.

http://www.innerchildpress.com/jackie-davis-allen.php
jackiedavisallen.com

The Irish Poet

His pen bled Ireland's poetic blood,
True to his nature, his poems
Speak, even today, years later, long
After he passed away in 1939.

From an early age, influenced
By the poet Shelly, in his teens,
He wrote; and at age 24, finally
He was published.

Some may say, "Oh, he had privileges,
His family was wealthy, his brother a painter,
His sister, involved in the arts and crafts".
No one can take away his gifts, then or now.

At the age of 58, in 1923, Yates, poet, mystic, Senator,
Protestant, won the Nobel Prize for literature.

Prelude to the Coronation

O ancient star of gold
You sparkle on the silvery mesh
Of morning's frosty breath
While dripping crystals of icy white
Clinging to branches of budding coins,
And in the wake of melting banks
Of snow, seasonal treasures of
Emerald and amethyst glow.
Brilliant sunbeams streaming down
On gilded keys, unlocking petals of ivory
You awaken wine kissed dreams, while
Suddenly, from branches of ebony
Sparkling splashes of sapphire and ruby
Streak across the azure sky
And, Spring, revealed in all her glory,
Returns and reigns on Winter's sigh!
O ancient star of gold
Sparkling on silvery mesh
A treasured note, frosty cold, I confess,
I often refresh the meter of my crystal lines
I shudder to realize, to know
Like butterflies in which you so delight
Emeralds and amethyst now do glow
Emerging in truth, both day and night
Still you dance on gilded keys
While I am tormented by recurring dreams
Of long hidden sapphires and rubies
You now perfume with wine kissed themes.

O ancient star of gold, you steal my story!
Yet, another day I'll take back by glory!

Jackie Davis Allen

Respite in the Midst of the Storm

Could it be that this earth drenching
is the way the Master Gardner gets our attention
to give us an excuse?
And, if you will,
to take time out from our routine
to do some of the things
we've found ourselves saying?
"I wish I had the time to.....
.

The storm continues,
pittering and pattering, pittering and pattering
tap, tap, tapping splash, splash, splashing.
Boom, boom, booming, crash crashing!
Blast blasting, and clap, clap clapping!
The evening screams! Shrieks! A brilliant white lightning
ignites the darkness of the night!
Still, I continue to write, my paper accepting the words.

The reflection of the wet exuberance
of nature is all around me.
My breath fogs the cloudy windowpane;
A thunderous voice announces!
"Impending is the new birth! A greening of the earth"!
And as for me, my muse hovers around.

The flickering candle, with a swoosh of air
is extinguished as I venture to open the door.
I breathe in the night's gift, hesitant
to retire to my cozy bedroom. My thoughts continue,
accompanied by the heaven's outpouring.
Pitter, patter, pat, pat, tap tap, splash, boom, crash!
The wet of the noisy night goes on! And, on!

Tzemin Ition Tsai

Tzemin Ition Tsai

Dr. Tzemin Ition Tsai comes from the Republic of China(Taiwan). In addition to being a professor of literature at a university, he is more committed to writing poems, novels, and proses. He is also an editor of "Reading, Writing and Teaching" academic text, an International editor of "Contemporary dialogues" literary periodical in Macedonia, and Vice-Chairman of the International Jury of the SAHITTO INTERNATIONAL AWARD in Bangladesh, and a columnist for "Chinese Language Monthly" in Taiwan.

In a wide range of literary creations, he is particularly fond of interesting stories or novels, and writing articles or poems about the feelings of nature and human beings. He has won many national literary awards. His literary works have been anthologized and published in books, journals, and newspapers in more than 55 countries and have been translated into more than 24 languages.

Cold Stone Anvil Under the Autumn Moon

In the stillness of autumn night, the bright moon hangs in the arching cosmos,
Casting its clear lustrous light upon the ancient window and speckled antique desk.
A sense of desolation surrounds, with absolute silence falling upon all things, evoking an air of melancholy.

The distant clanging of the stone anvil, now breaking now continuing,
Flows with the dying autumn breeze, dances with the descending fallen leaves.
This mysterious rhythm is dreamlike, like a melody from another world.

While the neighbors have rested, I stand guard with my solitary lamp,
Leaning against the window, listening to the silent conversations of nocturnal geese.
It seems to echo the heartbeat of the universe,
Or perhaps the whispers of old companions.

Beneath the moon, I sift through each word,
Attempting to weave tales of the past into a fresh prose,
Yet the words are like scattered jewels,
Each falling to the ground, too resistant to form a poem.

Ah, the cold stone anvil under the autumn moon, to whom would play and probe it once more?
Does it lament the forgetfulness of passing years, or nursed an unfinished sentiment?
Or could it be the tearful sigh of autumn's end,
Leaving behind only the grievances of the lonely deep night.

Dance of the Soul

In the canopy of the heavens, a frozen stare hangs upon the limitless thread,
The millennia-old mountains in their tranquility, scrawl the tale of the passage of time with each step of the sojourner.
As if time's silken strands slide through the eye of destiny's needle,
Beside the coursing rivers, spirits stand sentinel beneath age-old arboreal sentinels.
In the veins of the sapient, the blossoming of flowers signifies nothing more than fleeting moments of dazzle.
Silently through a season, leaf upon leaf reel in the dance.
We emerge from a particle of dust and in the end, must dissolve into the wind
Star-shaped chessboard, dreams are steered by the illumination from the heart
In the expansive theatre of nature, fleeting visitors master the art of the mountain's stoic face.
Signposting the serpentine path of rivers, between the solemnity of cosmos and desolation.
Staring at our own reflection, we are minuscule yet shimmer like cosmic bodies.
In the woodlands, the whispering wind mutters,
Striving to rouse the liberty of my designated soul.
This piece of wilderness, the primordial scriptures between heaven and earth.
In the twilight of the setting sun, the seeds of wisdom,
Are chronicled in every single step of the journey, archived like poems of our miracles.
Within my own being, the instantaneous breath of awakening has long been awaiting.

The Night Lamp Remains

As night falls, silence descends, and the lamp stands alone.
In the darkness it seeks the embrace of solitude,
The copper glow of the lamp on the mountainside reflects the past, lingering like smoke,
The dim light of the lamp gently caresses the passage of time,
Each flicker, a stirring of the soul.

Through the shattered window it draws the moonlight in a myriad of colors,
Where the heart leads, let the years cut and reassemble,
The night traveler asks, where is the way home?

Steps are lost, the night echoes the search in vain,
The lamp remains silent, silently symbolizing the philosophy of life,
In the emptiness, the lamp is soft, humming,
In the silence we explore the beginning and the end of life,

History is being written, ink is flowing like a river,
Each ray of light, wavering,
Reflecting on itself over and over, wandering in the labyrinth of the night,
The night has seeped into the bones, the heart's journey has returned to the sky,
The lamp perseveres, the weak light maintains the remaining power of the residual oil.
Contemplation with only a remnant of the night,
At dawn, guiding until the morning light washes away.

Shareef Abdur Rasheed

Shareef Abdur Rasheed

Shareef Abdur-Rasheed, AKA Zakir Flo was born and raised in Brooklyn, New York. His education includes Brooklyn College, Suffolk County Community College and Makkah, Saudi Arabia. He is a Veteran of the Viet Nam era, where in 1969 he reverted to his now reverently embraced Islamic Faith. He is very active in the Islamic community and beyond with his teachings, activism and his humanity.

Shareef's spiritual expression comes through the persona of "Zakir Flo". Zakir is Arabic for "To remind". Never silent, Shareef Abdur-Rasheed is always dropping science, love, consciousness and signs of the time in rhyme.

Shareef is the Patriarch of the Abdur-Rasheed Family with 9 Children (6 Sons and 3 Daughters) and 41 Grandchildren (24 Boys and 17 Girls).

For more information about Shareef, visit his personal FaceBook Page at :

https://www.facebook.com/shareef.abdurrasheed1
https://zakirflo.wordpress.com

William Butler Yeats

B: 13 June 1865
D: 28 January 1939
one of the great artists
of his time
major influence
literature
20th century
Nobel prize literature
1923 recipient
certainly, one the most
highly regarded artist
Ireland produced
his poetry went through
transitions impacted
by the social/political
reality of the times
certainly, the advent
of the 20th century
and its global constant
growth as regards
modernism, social/
political unrest
world war,
certainly, Irish domestic
issues had great affect
on his work which
addressed the reality
of mortality
death was always
stalking
to appreciate every
breath to say the very

least a under statement
that dominated his
appreciation of life
reflected in his artistic
expressions
one of the greats of his
time
long live his work

fragments only..,

what was left
of humanity
trickled down
around me
i thought certainly
things not what
they used to be
where is humanity?
many who appear
to be
turns out not to be
apparently
sincerity scarcity
feelings seemed empty
searched obituary
looked for humanity
didn't see
went to cemetery
read stones
what goes?
seemed humanity
was gone
chill covered me
to think no humanity
how can one live free,
what's to become of me?
i cried for mankind
realized when i cried
humanity hadn't died
it's still alive in me
hope remains
eternally rains

Bling
----

got your nose?
remember!
all that glitters ain't gold
as the "ol" saying goes
even gold loses value
just as what glitters
turns out to be hollow
hot today is
cold tomorrow
elation becomes deflation
joy becomes sorrow
when we're taken in by
glittering bling today
became a withering thing
tomorrow
even a rose that's fresh
soon crumbles
so goes health and wealth
all signs designed to
remind
help keep us humble
does here today gone
tomorrow equal
life eternal
free of pain, sorrow?
remember..,
glitters value is zero
in the grave
where the only legal tender
to negotiate
is righteous deeds
performed by the slave

Shareef Abdur Rasheed

that he or she gave
with pure intention
hearts clean
in surrender
only to please their lord
being the only endeavor
who with undeserved mercy
bestowed never owed
admits them into gardens
where beneath rivers flow
where they will dwell forever
fact is that's real, is bling?
never!

Noreen Snyder

Noreen Snyder

Noreen Ann Snyder has been writing since she was a teenager. She writes a variety of different topics. Her favorite poetic forms are Sonnets, Blitz, Haiku, Tanka, and Free Verse. She always learning different poetic forms.

Noreen Ann Snyder is a poet, writer, and an author of five books, (four books are co-authored with her late husband, Garry A. Snyder.) Her poetry is in several Inner Child Press Anthologies. She is the founder of The Poetry Club on Facebook.

William Butler Yeats

Yeats, an outstanding poet,
one of the greatest poets of 20th century,
the Nobel Prize in Literature 1923 winner
and the first Irish person to do so,
the writer of many colors,
diversified poetry
about love, religion, politics, social class,
family, and so many many more.
He is very talented, gifted, fascinating,
interesting poet and writer
who has captivated readers from around the world
and always will.

Our Home (Haiku)

Filled with love, joy, peace

filled with memories-good, bad

the best place to be.

A Live Orchestra

When the sky dances

and colors sing,

thunder roars,

and the lightening flashes

like watching the Heavenly orchestra.

I know you're playing your guitar in Heaven,

serenading me

as Angels pluck their harps.

Wishing for wings,

so I can fly,

watch and hear you in person

like a live orchestra on a Heavenly stage.

Elizabeth E. Castillo

Elizabeth Esguerra Castillo

Elizabeth Esguerra Castillo is a multi-awarded and an Internationally-Published Contemporary Author/Poet and a Professional Writer / Creative Writer / Feature Writer / Journalist / Travel Writer from the Philippines. She has 2 published books, "Seasons of Emotions" (UK) and "Inner Reflections of the Muse", (USA). Elizabeth is also a co-author to more than 60 international anthologies in the USA, Canada, UK, Romania, India. She is a Contributing Editor of Inner Child Magazine, USA and an Advisory Board Member of Reflection Magazine, an international literary magazine. She is a member of the American Authors Association (AAA) and PEN International.

Web links:

Facebook Fan Page

https://free.facebook.com/ElizabethEsguerraCastillo

Google Plus

https://plus.google.com/u/0/+ElizabethCastillo

The Immortal Yeats

His verses are immortal,

Will be admired 'til the end of time

Like "Leda and the Swan", his lines caress the soul

Even the Uninvited Guest "Death" finds them sublime.

Like a falcon, with keen eyes

His "Second Coming" is a passionate depiction

Spiritual, awakening, and apocalyptic

"He Wishes for the Cloths of Heaven",

An intricate play of words yearning for richness.

Stigmata

He carries the weight of the world upon His shoulders,
Gave up His life for Man's redemption
Sacrificed His own blood to save the world
And for sins to be forgiven,
These deep wounds appearing on the palm of my hands
Symbolic of the stigmata inflicted on His pitiful body
The vortex of life ebbed at the center
Signifying a new life, the dawning of a new tomorrow.

My Calling

Have you discovered your Highest Calling?
The True Purpose of your birth upon the Earth
Some might still be roaming around in circles
Still not finding the answers which are just within themselves.
It comes, it appears like a thief in the night
You just wake up one day and boom!
Everything clicks!
You find yourself doing things that you love ever since you were a kid
The kid who dreamed, the innocent soul who once imagined herself to become someone,
'Til doors were opened, windows welcomed her
And triumphantly exclaims: "This is my calling!"

Mutawaf Shaheed

Mutawaf Shaheed

C. E. Shy has been writing since the seventh grade. He continued writing through high school, until he became more involved in sports. After his graduation, he worked at the White Motors Company where he wrote for the company's newspaper. He started a column called: "The Poet's Corner." That was his first published work.

www.innerchildpress.com/c-e-shy.php

At the Gates

Clearing hidden paths that block the gates.
Not much time to enunciate.
Using the letters as counter weights.
Making certain the message resonates to those who are unfortunate.
Probing the uncertainties that lie ahead.
Some of those things I may love, some of them I may dread.
Being one of those who forge ahead.
Speaking for the living and the dead.

Many things can't be seen, but can be said.
In the works done by me will be read.
Stretching out as far as I can.
The ultimate of all understanding is in no man's hand.
Stranded at the liberation station waiting to finish the ride.

Dilemma

Will it be lemon, lime or lavender?
What will the lady like? It might make
her like me even more, if her common
scents know my intentions.

I think the ladies can arrive at conclusions,
when bro man can't see anything coming.
Should it be brown, blue or a different
shade of gray?

Green is for the grass and leaves, when
they please the summer seasons. Wow
I forgot to get my things out the cleaners.
I guess these faded jeans will have to do.

Apples, peaches, pears or plums? She will
be impressed when she comes. Table cloth
or placement mats?

You think she will pay any attention to that?
I'll bring out my dog and put away my cat.
She said, she had a gift to give my Pitbull
Rex.

I don't have time to wash the windows today.
I'll just close them and pull down the blinds.
The doorbell rings, and she steps inside.
I hand her flowers and she started to sneeze.

Her blue contacts came loose, the extensions
fell off and the eyelashes too. A few minutes
later, I asked, "who the hell are you?"

Mutawaf Shaheed

She pressed on her nails trying to get them
to stick. She shook her fist, and had this to say,
"you must take this, for I have no other kind."

Private Bedlam

When she entered the room,
he had I quit on his face.
There was nothing available
to resist her. There was no
defense against her
determination.

He knew the closer she came,
the less he could restrain
himself. She made up her
mind that she was coming
after him and there was no
place to run.

Her beauty disabled him.
He saw her before at the
grocery store. She smiled
at him once at the gym.

He thought how unfair it
was that she could so
easily take advantage of
him.

He felt so common and
unattractive when she
was around him. Why
would she wants to be
with him?

She had the ability to bring
that out in a man. Her smile

Mutawaf Shaheed

was a command. The way she
walked, it said, "I run this!"

He shouldn't have accepted
the invitation to the bedlam
show! He finally was able
to escape though a broken
window in his mind. He never
thought of her again, that was
the only way to win.

hülya n. yılmaz

hülya n. yılmaz

Of Turkish descent, hülya n. yılmaz [sic] is Professor Emerita (Penn State, U.S.A.), Director of Editing Services (Inner Child Press International, U.S.A.), and a trilingual literary translator. Before her poetry and prose publications, she authored an extensive research book in German on cross-cultural literary influences.

Her works of literature include a trilingual collection of poems, memoirs in verse, prose poetry, short stories, a bilingual poetry book, and two books of poetry (one, co-authored). Her poetic offerings appeared in numerous anthologies of global endeavors.

hülya writes creatively to attain and nourish a comprehensive awareness for and development of our humanity.

hülya n. yılmaz, a traveler on the journey called "life" . . .

Writing Web Site
https://hulyanyilmaz.com/

Editing Web Site
https://hulyasfreelancing.com

fin de siècle

late 19th century
Germany, France, England, Austria,
along with others . . .

extreme aestheticism
fashionable despair
world-weariness
sophistication
escapism

self-appointed
self-assessed

elitist?

Yeats' Prayer for His Daughter

Like an ordinary person,
Yeats voices parental wishes
for his newborn in his fatherly existence.

"A Prayer for My Daughter",
he names his modernist poem.
His hopes and expectations galore.

A definition of a woman-to-be
and visions of a happy life for his offspring
emerge lovingly from his poetic construct.

Heartfelt
like an ordinary person . . .

hülya n. yılmaz

escapism

emotions run high

meander in nature then

breathe in her dazzle

Teresa E. Gallion

Teresa E. Gallion

Teresa E. Gallion was born in Shreveport, Louisiana and moved to Illinois at the age of 15. She completed her undergraduate training at the University of Illinois Chicago and received her master's degree in Psychology from Bowling Green State University in Ohio. She retired from New Mexico state government in 2012.

She moved to New Mexico in 1987. While writing sporadically for many years, in 1998 she started reading her work in the local Albuquerque poetry community. She has been a featured reader at local coffee houses, bookstores, art galleries, museums, libraries, Outpost Performance Space, the Route 66 Festival in 2001 and the State of Oklahoma's Poetry Festival in Cheyenne, Oklahoma in 2004. She occasionally hosts an open mic.

Teresa's work is published in numerous Journals and anthologies. She has two CDs: *On the Wings of the Wind* and *Poems from Chasing Light*. She has published three books: *Walking Sacred Ground, Contemplation in the High Desert* and *Chasing Light*.

Chasing Light was a finalist in the 2013 New Mexico/Arizona Book Awards.

The surreal high desert landscape and her personal spiritual journey influence the writing of this Albuquerque poet. When she is not writing, she is committed to hiking the enchanted landscapes of New Mexico. You may preview her work at

http://bit.ly/1aIVPNq or *http://bit.ly/13IMLGh*

Teresa E. Gallion

Homage to Yeats

Reading your biography
tells a tale of humble beginnings,
difficulty with math and languages.
Possibly because of dyslexia
and tone deafness.

Greatness often emerges from humility.
Not schooled in the formalities of writing,
your pen spoke to you at the
tender age of 17. You developed
and expanded into a master writer.

Your creative legacy was given
a Nobel Prize in literature and
recognition as a major 20th century
English language poet.

You are identified as a Symbolist poet
who uses allusive imagery and symbolic
structures throughout your work.
A timeless quality in the eyes of many.

Slow Ascent

They play in the elysian fields.
His beautiful fur balls of black and white
and her delicate bare feet
massage blades of grass.

Eternal flames streak across
the heavenly planes,
exposes naked healing.
She lets go of painfulness.

The longing that weighs
heavy on her soul rolls away.
Her fur baby purrs a love song
in praise of freedom.

Shadows close the veil
of sadness around her soul.
Joy makes love to her smile.
She tenderly squeezes her big love.

Teresa E. Gallion

Open Arms

When you learn to swim
through waves of pain,
you are on the path
to freedom to be you.

Let all your healing bleed
on the blank space.
Climb the white walls
of your writing room
and smack the ceiling
with word power.
Watch a stream
of lines reach for the floor.

Now sweep them into stanzas
with your delicate broom straws.
Let them float around the room.
You have entered the place
of imagery and amazement
where flowers bloom from words.

Water has no remorse for those
who bathe in need of purification.
Come hither and float
in the pure flow of lyrics.
When you are ready,
I will take you to the writer's lodge.

Ashok K. Bhargava

Ashok K. Bhargava

ASHOK BHARGAVA is a poet, writer, inspirational speaker and a literary consultant. He has attended poetry conferences in Italy, Turkey, India and Philippines. His latest book "Riding the Tide" about his battle with cancer has been translated and published in Arabic, Hindi, Telugu and Bengali languages. He is a contributing writer to several anthologies worldwide including World Poetry Almanac 2014. He has been published in numerous print and online magazines.

Ashok has won many accolades including Poet Ambassador to Japan, Kalidasa International award, World Poetry Lifetime Achievement award, Writers Beyond Borders Peace award and Tapsilog Leadership award for his community involvement. He is founder of Writers International Network Canada Society to discover, nourish, recognize and celebrate writers, poets and artists and to assist them to network with the community at large. He is the author of eight books of poetry and one anthology. He is Artist-in-Residence at Moberly Arts & Cultural Centre and also co-edits the literary section of The Link Newspaper.

Light of a Flame / Symbolism

For William Butler Yeats

What is unsaid speaks louder, clearer and
paints vivid images of the unseen

wind among the reeds
appealing the spirits to talk.

Every present moment
perpetuates the unknown

between the earth and the sky
pulsating with mysticism.

It's an idea waiting to be uttered
to fill the empty souls with

the brightness of the verse
with perpetual virginity of the soul.

Light

Your soft beam touches
my bare loneliness

a cool-wave embrace
of a Milky Way.

You are a moon
that shows dark specks

devoid of innocent
bright light.

I am hope:
a crush of crushed

bones
underneath the skin.

In the end we are only
tiny particles of light
not the reflection
on the river surface.

We are shards of light
torn and broken

unafraid
of darkness.

The path to go back to home
is not out there, it is inside the heart.

In Search of Eternal Life

The water of Ganga
Failed to wash my sins
Yet just few drinks of whisky
Washed them clean and
Mortification of flesh
Nurtured divinity in me
But why the heart of a man
Keeps changing.

Rain follows rain
Nights are long
I wake up
Drowsy eyes in the morning
Flowers fresh from the night rain
Give off sweet fragrance
Raindrops on the grass smile
Ah that is a beautiful life

poetry
recitals
sweet gatherings

are a source of light
that burns
quietly
eagerly
to enter us
when we are ready

and then it shines
inside of us with
a lucid revelation
of deep love

to light up the marvelous
pleasures
like a full moon

Ashok K. Bhargava

Caroline
'Ceri Naz'
Nazareno
Gabis

Caroline 'Ceri' Nazareno-Gabis

Caroline 'Ceri Naz' Nazareno-Gabis, author of Velvet Passions of Calibrated Quarks, World Poetry Canada International Director to Philippines is a multi-awarded poet, editor, journalist, educator, peace and women's advocate. She believes that learning other's language and culture is a doorway to wisdom.

Among her poetic belts include **Gabrielle Galloni Memorial Panorama International Youth Award** 2022, Panorama Youth Literary Awards 2020, 7th Prize Winner in the 19th, 20th and 21st Italian Award of Literary Festival; Writers International Network-Canada ''Amazing Poet 2015'', The Frang Bardhi Literary Prize 2014 (Albania), Poet Journalist Award 2014 (Tuzla, Istanbul, Turkey) and World Poetry Empowered Poet 2013 (Vancouver, Canada). She's a featured member of Association of Women's Rights and Development (AWID), The Poetry Posse, Galaktika Poetike, Asia Pacific Writers and Translators (APWT), Axlepino and Anacbanua. Her poetry and children's stories have been featured in different anthologies and magazines worldwide.

Links to her works:

http://panitikan.ph/2018/03/30/caroline-nazareno-gabis/

https://apwriters.org/author/ceri_naz/

http://www.aveviajera.org/nacionesunidasdelasletras/id1181.html

Castles and Queens
(A response to William B. Yeats)

When the sun shines over a woman's face

Her beauty radiates throughout

Beyond the world or words;

Describing every strand of her hair

Ageing gracefully,

Her crown over the fields of memories,

Castles of her achievements

From storm to storm;

Her mind is a theater of purpose,

Where her talents are curtains of victorious laments

From the breaking dawn to the dusk,

She is alive,

The queen of greatest play!

The Rain Keeps Falling

every time i hold a glass of water,

i think of its every drop,

its mild dew kissing

the surface of the glass,

I think it can rinse trepidation,

The tears of joy and of pain,

for now, waiting for the rain

so all dark matters

could be drowned in the abyss.

Caroline 'Ceri' Nazareno-Gabis

Walls

Sometimes, life is so hard
That it pushes you back,
Sometimes, you cry over it,
Trying to break free,
It becomes a mimicry,
Of lonesome spirit,
When the light streaks get in,
There is hope in every wall,
Walls divide us,
When the heart doesn't recognize
Your presence and worth.

Swapna Behera

Swapna Behera

Swapna Behera is a trilingual poet, translator, environmentalist, editor from India and author of seven books of different genres including one on children's literature on Environment. She is the recipient of International UGADI AWARD 2019, honoured from Gujurat Sahitya Akademi 2022, 2021 International Poesis Award of Honor as Jury, Pentasi B World Fellow Poet, Honoured Poet of India from Seychelles Government and International awards from Algeria, Morocco, Kajhakhstan, modern Arabic Literary Renaissance of Egypt, International Arts Council Argentina etc. Her stories, poems, articles are published in many International and National magazines and ezines. Her poem A NIGHT IN THE REFUGEE CAMP is translated into 67 languages. She has received over 60 National and International Awards. At present she is the Cultural Ambassador for India and South Asia of Inner Child and the life member of Odisha Environmental Society

Email
swapna.behera@gmail.com

Web Site
http://swapnabehera.in/

William Butler Yeats

the Irish poet and politician

his poems rhythmic and structured

vigorous and direct

evocative symbols he used

the rose, bird, wheel,

tree, water, air, fire or tower

the first Irish noble laureate in literature

whose popular modernist work

"A prayer for my daughter"

masterpiece is his poem "The second coming"

a senator and founder of Irish literary theatre

who rides with fairies upon the wind

and dances upon the mountain like a flame

that's why I say, come

that's why I say
please come to my
vintage village
you can see the bone marrows
carrying the forest
the flowing river with fresh water
sprinkle myriads of aboriginal knowledge
here or there
segments are fragile
ligaments are broken
but yet the soil whispers
lo behold
here winks the new dawn
the straight line of the spine is bent
carrying the basket of grains
the farmer knows where to sow the seeds
when to harvest
how to preserve grains for future
the ants, honeybees
carry the spring fire on their back
the dimples of the carnival
celebrate the season's breathe
who creates Gods?
that's why I say
please come and feel HIS presence
I think man creates God

thunder, blunder and wonder

he said "I married a wonder woman"
she washes, cooks, teaches, cleans
takes care of family, doggie and garden
saves money, water, electricity
travels in public transport
she is the jewel who smiles all the way to solve
she knows to love
she is the wonder woman
he said "I married a thunder woman"
who shouts, screams
never tolerates indiscipline
she divides the work
she earns, takes an off day and rests
pampers herself, celebrates her entity
a crisis manager she is
each member follows her stricture
she is the thunder woman
he said "I have no wife"
she died last year
each night she is crucified on the bed
her purse is empty always
she never demands
so do we never think about
her sickness or her needs
her voice is silent
last night she committed suicide
the children lost a mother
the man planned to get another girl
she is the blunder woman
three women on the stage
three perceptions towards life
dignity; thou art the common agenda for all

Albert 'Infinite' Carrasco

Albert 'Infinite' Carassco

Albert "Infinite The Poet" Carrasco is an urban poet, mentor and public speaker.

Albert believes his experience of growing up in poverty, dealing with drugs and witnessing murder over and over were lessons learnt, in order to gain knowledge to teach. Albert's harsh reality and honesty is a powerfully packed punch delivered through rhyme. Infinite grew up in the east part of the Bronx and still resides there, so he knows many young men will follow the same dark path he followed looking for change. The life of crime should never be an option to being poor but it is, very often.

Infinite poetry @lulu.com

Alcarrasco2 on YouTube

Infinite the poet on reverbnation

Infinite Poetry

www.lulu.com/us/en/shop/al-infinite-carrasco/infinite-poetry/paperback/product-21040240.html

www.innerchildpress.com/albert-carrasco

William Butler Yeats

I am a Irish poet, dramatist and writer,
In fact my work made me one of the foremost figures of 20th century literature,
I was a driving force of the Irish literary revival and a founder of the Abby Theatre.
Poetry was something I loved at an early age, I always wanted to see my name on a book or speak to the masses as I grace a stage.
I wanted to be like my Dad in some way, he painted pictures and portraits,
So did I, the difference between him and me was that I painted mental pictures, as a poet.
Art ran in the family, my brother painted and my sisters were crafty.
In 1923 I was awarded the Nobel peace prize in literature, then right after I became an Irish free state senator.
I was a fierce opponent of individualism and political liberalism,
I'd rather have nationalist leadership and an authoritarian system.
My views were express through music, acting, dance, in congress, especially through poetry

Bx Slums

It's been two decades since I started tapping keys, sharpening pencils to meet my mind specs and leaving traces of pen ink across paper. my forte is well known... poverty, drugs, jail and murder. I'm in my own lane, it's an Audubon of happiness and hurt paved by joy and pain. Infinite is one of a few that remain from the birth circa of the game who soaked in sun rays, witnessed three days of blood rain and lifetime sentences ending trap reigns. I chose to write and spit scars in the form of urban poetic bars to enlighten those that are out here chasn fast money, fast women and fast cars, I was there, I was with many men yelln out...the world is ours. When I'm in my zone I'm digging deep to memory hone, so much runs through my head... hunger, money, fun, laughter, then disaster, football numbers and flowers for the dead. I see red, written words are how I tear shed, for others it's wisdom being spread. I drop jewels for diamonds in the rough whom will most likely lose their shine to caskets and cuffs. I still be in trenches, nothing changed but the players wanting necks and wrist to drip vvs's. History will constantly repeat, mistakes aren't learnt from, I could spit a piece from 08 written bout the 80's run and it'll sound as if I wrote it today about life in these BX slums

Agony

The agony, the pain, after they pulled the trigger this is what the bullet rang after the bang, as It twirls like little ballerina girls, its searching for death, or the best thing next, like being a veggy or paraplegic, a wheelchair is detrimental, when feet have no use for walking on cement, or after being bullet riddled we become bed ridden, with a tube leading to a bag, for us to piss and shit in. If we do walk again after the hot spirally object impacts, we may walk with limps, or with a set of crutches for amputated limbs, or a walker with tennis balls on the ends so we don't slip. Burn marks mark our body from every bullet that left a clip. I tried to tattoo over what guns do, if you look you can't tell, but if you touch your feel rugged epidermis where the bullets went through, they protrude. When its foggy or it rains, I got a slug by my lung, on these days I feel the most pain, they say they spray with no names, not this day I was the indented target to this lame, he called a queen out her name, so I came with the knuckle game like Mosley, next thing you know he pulled the trigger, the bullet rang after the bang, that sucker left me with 4 holes staggering into emergency, they started flushing me, lead poison testing me, it was a 50 50 chance to live if they operated me, I was only 16, moms chose to opt out of surgery on me. To the street world I am now an outsider, but inside me ill forever have a street life reminder.

Michelle Joan Barulich

Michelle Joan Barulich

Michelle Joan Barulich was born in Honolulu, Hawaii on the island of Oahu. She started writing poetry and songs with her younger brother Paul. They have written many songs in their teen years. She is currently studying Alternative Medicine and would like to become a Homeopathic Doctor. Michelle loves all kinds of animals and birds; she does wild rehabilitation. She has also rescued rock pigeons that make great pets.

https://www.facebook.com/michelle.barulich

Michelle Joan Barulich

Dear William

Dear William, what a driving force you were

from poet to writer to winning the Nobel Prize in Literature

You were a symbolist poet

Using imagery and abstracts thoughts

Your books and poems are still in demand

Your words, your thoughts, and your poems

Will always remain timeless treasures.

Inside the Light

Growing up in this world
Was very hard to take
But growing up in the future
Will be much harder to make
I see no doors open for me
Chances are they are locked
I see no keys being handed to me
Because the boats in the harbor are docked
Inside the lights
Holds nightmares for me
Inside the light death is all I see
Inside the light I'm reaching in
Where happiness is something, people have to lend
Sitting in silence in my room
I'm reaching the end
Where happiness something people have to pretend.

Middle Ground

All I wanted was some time
Some time, to sort things in my mind
We were once young and free
 Didn't have to look back
Now, every day that approaches me
I find myself lost
Found out that there is no middle ground
Walking down the isolated road
Finding myself choosing once again
Walking down the deserted road
I hear my lover call
We were once young and free
 I find myself lost
Found out there is no middle ground
All I need is some time
Some time, to make up my mind
Finding myself standing upon the middle ground now
We were once young and free
Didn't have to look back at all.

Eliza Segiet

Eliza Segiet

Eliza Segiet graduated with a Master's Degree in Philosophy at Jagiellonian University.

Received *Global Literature Guardian Award* – from Motivational Strips, World Nations Writers Union and Union Hispanomundial De Escritores (UHE) 2018.

Nominated for the Pushcart Prize 2019, 2021.

Laureate *Naji Naaman Literary Prize 2020*,

International Award Paragon of Hope (2020),

World Award 2020 *Cesar Vallejo* for Literary Excellence. Laureate of the Special Jury *Sahitto International Award* 2021, World Award *Premiul Fănuş Neagu* 2021.

Finalist *Golden Aster Book* World Literary Prize 2020, *Mili Dueli* 2022, Voci nel deserto 2022.

At the international Festival of Poetry CAMPIONATO MONDIALE DI POESIA (2021/2022) she won the title of vice-champion of the world.

Award BHARAT RATNA RABINDRANATH TAGORE INTERNATIONAL AWARD (2022).

Award - *World Poets Association* (2023).

Laureate Between words and infinity *"International Literary Award (2023)*.

Eliza Segiet

Saving the World
In memory of William Butler Yeats

The purity of the moon,
the enchanting sounds
were the light of his imagination.
He believed
that dormant thoughts were better awakened
when music merged with them.
Fascinated by mythology,
he was capable of reviving history
and saving the world with words.

The eternity of stone,
of which he wrote,
is the anchor
around which
history takes place.
And he, despite the horror that surrounded him,
is a symbol of the strength of heart.

*William Butler Yeats is considered one of the greatest poets of the 20th century. He represented to the Protestant Anglo-Irish minority.

Translated by Dorota Stępińska

Tangles

Memories rustle in her,
but she knows
he is where he belongs –
with the one he doesn't love
but is with,
with the one
he cheats on.

Bathed, rested,
ready for new experiences,
every day
he went out to handle affairs.

She doesn't want to be the second,
third, or next one anymore…

Memories remain
– those tangles of common time
and regret that
he always went back to where
he came from.

He was everything to her,
she
– a variety to the monotony.

Translated by Artur Komoter

Contours

Now
they don't need anything from her,
they have no reason to call
after all
she could always manage,
and they
– are fine without her.

Once again, she understood
that friendship
was an illusion.

After the years, she remembers
only the contours
of hands outstretched in need.

Once,
the sound of the phone
cut through her silence,
now
– only she remains.

Translated by Artur Komoter

William S. Peters Sr.

William S. Peters, Sr.

Bill's writing career spans a period of well over 50 years. Being first Published in 1972, Bill has since went on to Author in excess of 50+ additional Volumes of Poetry, Short Stories, etc., expressing his thoughts on matters of the Heart, Spirit, Consciousness and Humanity. His primary focus is that of Love, Peace and Understanding!

Bill says . . .

I have always likened Life to that of a Garden. So, for me, Life is simply about the Seeds we Sow and Nourish. All things we "Think and Do", will "Be" Cause and eventually manifest itself to being an "Effect" within our own personal "Existences" and "Experiences" . . . whether it be Fruit, Flowers, Weeds or Barren Landscapes! Bill highly regards the Fruits of his Labor and wishes that everyone would thus go on to plant "Lovely" Seeds on "Good Ground" in their own Gardens of Life!

to connect with Bill, he is all things Inner Child

www.iaminnerchild.com

Personal Web Site

www.iamjustbill.com

A poem to William

I like that name
And the fact, like me
He claims to be a poet,
Or is it the world
Who titles us as such?

Though I am not quite there,
I perhaps some day
Will be eulogized
As a significant wordsmith . . .
And perhaps not . . .

Is my vanity showing . . .
Well,
Just the same
I thank you William
For lending unto us that follow
Some guidance
As to what
Excellence looks like

All done

Convictionistically, she looked at me
And I knew I was condemned
By my own admission

My conundrums of innocence
Would not hold up in court,
And appeals and mercy
Were out of the question

I was waiting for a plea deal,
And she agreed
To allow me to live . . .
And I was thankful
…..
I was done for
. . .
All because I ate her Nutella
….
In my defense,
I did wash out the empty jar
And put it in the recycle bin . . .
…..
That's how I was caught!

   . . . maybe I should have taken the label off!

Church Styles

Some are frigid landscapes
Painted warmly upon the canvass,
Depicting hidden stories
Begging to come to life
In our consciousness

Others are balmy glimpses
Into the things
That move things
Within us

Trees and skies
Tell of our hopes perhaps
And the ever-present waters
Reminds us to not stagnate
Though we are deciphering
The colors offered

Nothing is quite acutely lucid,
And thus allows me,
The onlooker, admirer
Room for a little wiggle
In my imagination

Let us go to 'Church' now
And listen to the silence
Upon the canvass

April 2024 Featured Poets

~  ~

Hassanal Abdullah

Johny Takkedasila

Rajashree Mohapatra

Shirley Smothers

Hassanal Abdullah

Hassanal Abdullah

Hassanal Abdullah, a Bengli poet, translator, lyricist, editor, and critic, who was born in Bangladesh and has immigrated to United States in 1990. He introduced *Swatantra Sonnets*: seven-seven stanza pattern and abcdabc efgdefg rhyming scheme and authored over 50 books in different genres. His *Collected Poems* (in Bengali) has been published in two volumes (560 pages each) from Dhaka. Abdullah's poetry has been translated into eleven languages and he has been invited to International Poetry Festivals in Poland, Greece, China, India, Canada, Mexico, and Kenya. He is the editor of *Shabdaguchha*, an International Bilingual Poetry Magazine, celebrating 25 years of publication. Abdullah is the recipient of *Ianicious* International Prize of Klemens Janicki (2021) from Poland, the Homer European Medal of Poetry and Art (2016), and a translation grant from the Queens Council of the Arts (2019), New York. His work has been translated into eleven languages. He has been a New York City High School math and computer teacher since 1998.

Hassanal Abdullah

Swatantra Sonnet 111

The world trembles in fear of atomic fusions.
Splitting its rib of grief, and targeting humans,
the long-range missiles rumble for a faster speed.
Like erect-penises, wrecking huts and bunkers,
cowardly, they carry out immense explosions,
and continue blood thirst for children and women.
Modernism now giggles with incredible greed.

A protest rally, at which sheer anger smolders,
speeds up in a daunting possibility, though,
hunger, non-schooling, homelessness, and, in the realm
of poverty, the uprising power-mongers,
smartly put it out, and sit on the poor's shoulders.
Hence, the earth-hole erupting a blood-volcano—
warplanes dwell in its froth with ballistic emblem.

Swatantra Sonnet 154

I do urge you not to keep my dead body here.
Boarding me on birds' wings, please send me to the green
grass, where the bucolic paths run across as robes
into the gold-mouthed village of my boyhood-land.
The huge tree standing at the bank of the pond near
my house, still waiting to receive me. I have been
wanted, too, by the mango and banana groves,

boundless mustard flowers glittering like the stars,
guarded me for sixteen years, would kiss my body
at their palpable touch. Through my respiration,
moment by moment, I still feel them calling and
asking me to stay. On a dewy morning, birds
ease me down, soothe me with tailorbird's melody—
I'll stay forever in rural inspiration.

Hassanal Abdullah

Swatantra Sonnet 185

I have withdrawn myself after a surprise visit.
Still, a vertebral cry of life exits within
the essence of laughter and pain; baby's cradling—
rivers' ruffling—storm—lure and lawful ordeal;
eventful exuberance, more of what seems fit
is rage, unlimited seductive sex, and begin
the human pensive pleasure of manifold rattling . . .

Still, there is nothing specific about the tour.
Defeating million of sperms, leaving them behind,
it seems now, it is good to get to the ballroom
of success. Showing, knowing, and smelling to feel—
these trifling ruminations—arguments, and more,
saving me a cot in green to sleep with mankind
and then, granting me to vanish in a vacuum.

Johny Takkedasila

Johny Takkedasila

Johny Takkedasila is a popular young poet, storyteller, novelist, critic, translator, and editor. Apart from writing poetry, stories, novels, and criticism in Telugu, he also translates literature from different languages into Telugu and translates Telugu literature into Hindi and English.

So far, he has published 19 books. Two of his famous long poems are 'Y,' which focuses on the third gender, and 'Uri Madhyalo Bodrai,' which explores the female organ.

He wrote the first Telugu novel on gay community issues titled "Madi Daatani Mata." Additionally, he has written a novel on the Devadasi system called "Devudi Bharya" and a novel on illicit relationships titled "Ranku."

In 2023, he received the Central Sahitya Akademi Award for his Criticism book "Vivechani." Which contains 50 criticism essays on poetry, story books, novels and criticism.

He is also making significant contributions to children's literature. He has published a collection of stories addressing children's problems, the first Telugu novel on children's rights, and a criticism book on children's stories.

Johny Takkedasila

Need a New Vagina

Don't speak of love, let it be,
If there is no love, how can romance be found?
Only unsatisfied desires leave their mark,
Love changes as the seasons change.

Let's converse openly, what's the matter?
Not yesterday's love, let's not shatter.
I stated it openly, without disguise,
Yesterday's allure still gleams in our eyes.

New valleys, hills, what's this, my friend?
Let's talk openly, without amend.
Today we seek, without refrain,
A new vagina, breasts, and buttocks, the aim.

Why blame only men, let's not pretend,
Women too desire something fresh to mend.
Not yesterday's penis, let's discuss,
In the dark, bodies meet, no need to fuss.

This is the truth, Naked reality.

Private Part

Shouldn't I declare what I hold dear?
Why do they decide
What's embraced & denied within my skin?

I yearn for the freedom to voice my desires,
The liberty to converse about my physical form,
I demand the right to opine
About my sacred vagina and nurturing breasts.

Who grants them the authority to say
Which body may be seen, and which concealed?
Yes, I cherish my vagina and breasts,
What's amiss in that? Pray, tell me.
Who sanctioned this regime to prescribe
The scope and depth of discourse,
Enshrouding me, my words, and my essence
In shadows for ages unending?

Who are they to define
What remains hidden in my frame?

Your sweat, the decomposed semen,
Nerves that swell like water's fleeting bubbles and then burst—
This ode is dedicated to you,
The creators of histories, the chroniclers of words,
The bearers of truths, and authors of books,
Exploring my breasts, my vagina, my buttocks,
And myriad other facets of my existence.

In speech, in stride, in every breath,
Between parted fingers, nestled between my thighs,

Johny Takkedasila

Near the spectrum of hues between my bosom,
On the trimmed hairs, or the droplet clinging to my brow,
On my earlobes, on my toes... All hail to you
Who governs my corporeal vessel.

I yearn for discourse, not division,
For words and questions, not silence,
For comparisons, not mere symbols,
For resilience and birth, not surrender to death,
For existence, unadulterated and untamed.
I yearn for the freedom of my very breath,
Ultimately, I demand the rights to my entirety—
My organs, unshackled, complete, and free.

This is not merely a poem; it's a profound inquiry,
Not a tale of suffering, but a testament to our struggle.

When Do Bangles Break?

When I sprinkle water on my feet,
Eyes painted upon them,
If the sun scorches those painted eyes,
A wilderness of life within me will perish.

He hunted my body, from toe ring to nose pin,
Used and thrown like a corpse,
My navel, the region below, between my thighs,
Becomes a lifeless form.

When I sleep next to him at night,
Something enters me, an unbidden delight.
What's wrong if the work is done reluctantly?
Isn't decoration meant for your entry?

A bell rings in the distant space,
Immediately, it seems, someone shouts, "Allah o akbar."
Nearby, someone prays with grace,
"Oh Jesus, save my child,"

It's as heavy as lead in my ears,
Then it seems! Sources to deny.

When do bangles break, I wonder and ponder?
I am not seeking anyone's death;
Freedom from discrimination.

Change doesn't need axes and knives,
I should only have the right to my body.

Johny Takkedasila

Rajashree Mohapatra

Rajashree Mohapatra

Rajashree Mohapatra: Born in Odisha in India has received her master's degree in 'History' and 'Journalism and Mass Communication' from Utkal University, Odisha. She is a teacher by profession. Being a post graduate in' Environmental Education and Industrial Waste Management 'from Sambalpur University Odisha, she has devoted herself as a Social Activist for the cause of social justice, Environmental issues and human rights in remote areas through non-governmental organisations. Poetry, Painting and Journalism are her passions.

Rajashree Mohapatra

A Silver Line

A silver line of solitude
May weave wisdom and call for a high sublimation
A conflict surfaces
Between Compassion and hatred
When love needs to rest.

As time passes
Ripples in the lake fade
Evening goes dim and pale
A gloomy night approaches in profound silence
And prevents anything to be seen in the darkness.

The temple bells profusely cry
With chanting of sacred hymns
The scattered prayers rugs in the streets
 lead me into my trances.

Oh ! The Invisible mercy
Have I not sought you desperately
And awaited your kindness
Before I get caught in the gulf of fear.

Embedded Scar

Between the sea and the shoreline
A drop of water touches my feet
And dries up leaving scars behind.

Seems it evaporates to form a
Cloud of unspent love
In the azured sky over the head
And concentrates to head a storm
To downpour a few memories in stead.

A grain of sand swapping
With strong waves of attachment
Is embedded in the abyssal plain
At the base of a continental rise of jealousy and hatred.

Unaware of these I walked miles away
Indifferently, hallucinated under an unmerciful sun
Keeping the frozen ground of jealousy and hatred away.

Tides in mind and soul that rise and fall like waves
Do ever hunt like a vibration of love
 Oh Alas!
It is just a grandeur
Just as love in autumn or winter,
That dazzles with golden scopes.

Rajashree Mohapatra

Fire In Smoke

When a spark ignites a flame
Breath starts dancing in rhythm
Heart beats appear sacred
And the mind sings an emotional rhyme.

The shadows, the night and the spill of pain
Frame the words to compose the hymn
They convey what they intend to
And cast a shadow on my skin.

Half baked thoughts of a sea of tranquility
With lofty desires of tiny dreams
Fill my blank soul with sweetness of a beehive
And sitting by the window pane
I see a teasing moon
While the azured sky reminds me,
Glimpses of fire in mounds of
smoke may remain still alive.

Shirley Smothers

Shirley Smothers

Shirley Smothers is an amateur Poet, Writer, and Artist. She mostly writes short stories. Some of her short stories can be viewed at Shirley Smothers@storystar.com

Any Questions
Boop46@hotmail.com

The Price of Freedom

A ghostly image of a soldier
Stood in the background,
As a mother, a babe in her
Arms stood by a grave site.
She lowly whispered, "Father This is your
son, Son this is your Father.
He gave his life so that
Others might live."

She will raise this child without
the aid of others. This child will
Grow to be a strong man,
Because his mother is strong.

Who is this Woman in the Mirror

Who is this woman in the mirror?
When did her hair turn gray?
What happened to the young girl who
used to laugh and play?

Who is this woman in the mirror?
Where is the grace and charm?
What happened to the young girl who
used to play on the farm?

Who is this woman in the mirror?
When did these wrinkles appear
What happened to the young girl whose
parents used to call dear?
Who is this woman in the mirror.

Shirley Smothers

Poem Three

The Cat saw
the Rat, and the Rat saw
the Cat.

There was pursuit,
but the Rat outsmarted
the Cat.

"I'll bide my time," said
the Cat. "One day
I'll catch you MR. Rat."

What do you think about
that? Do you think the Cat will
catch the Rat? I hope not
Because the Rat is too cute
to be eaten by the Cat!

Remembering

our fallen soldiers of verse

Janet Perkins Caldwell
February 14, 1959 ~ September 20, 2016

Alan W. Jankowski
16 March 1961 ~ 10 March 2017

The Butterfly Effect

"IS" in effect

Inner Child Press

News

Published Books

by

Poetry Posse Members

We are so excited to share and announce a few of the current books, as well as the new and upcoming books of some of our Poetry Posse authors.

On the following pages we present to you ...

Inner Child Press News

Alicja Maria Kuberska
Jackie Davis Allen
Gail Weston Shazor
hülya n. yılmaz
Nizar Sartawi
Elizabeth E. Castillo
Faleeha Hassan
Fahredin Shehu
Kimberly Burnham
Caroline 'Ceri' Nazareno
Eliza Segiet
Teresa E. Gallion
William S. Peters, Sr.

Now Available
www.innerchildpress.com

The Year of the Poet XI ~ April 2024

Now Available
www.innerchildpress.com

Inner Child Press News

Unapologetically BLACK & Blues

william s. peters, sr.

Now Available
www.innerchildpress.com

The Year of the Poet XI ~ April 2024

Now Available
www.innerchildpress.com

Inner Child Press News

Now Available
www.innerchildpress.com

The Year of the Poet XI ~ April 2024

Now Available
www.innerchildpress.com

Inner Child Press News

Now Available
www.innerchildpress.com

The Year of the Poet XI ~ April 2024

Now Available
www.innerchildpress.com

Inner Child Press News

Now Available at
www.amazon.com/gp/product/B08MYL5B7S/ref=dbs_a_def_rwt_hsch_vapi_tkin_p1_i2

The Year of the Poet XI ~ April 2024

Now Available at
www.innerchildpress.com

Inner Child Press News

Now Available
www.innerchildpress.com

The Year of the Poet XI ~ April 2024

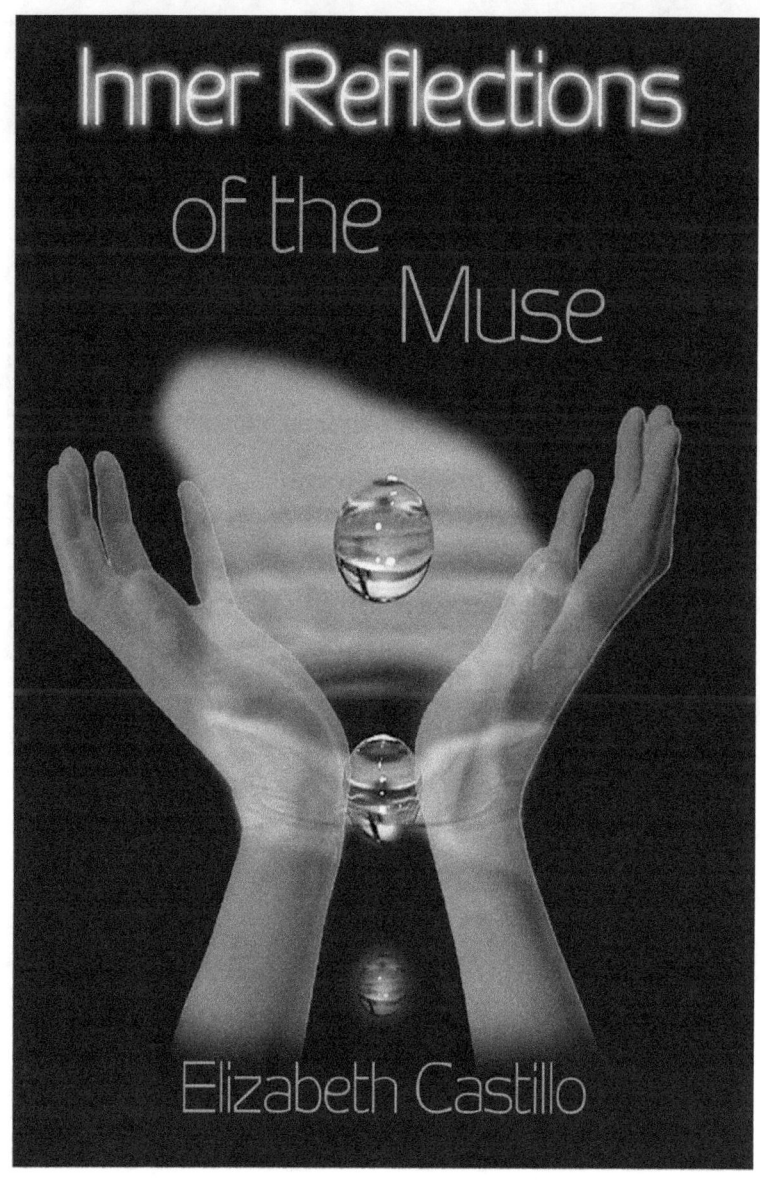

Now Available
www.innerchildpress.com

The Year of the Poet XI ~ April 2024

Now Available
www.innerchildpress.com

Inner Child Press News

Now Available
www.innerchildpress.com

The Year of the Poet XI ~ April 2024

The Book of krisar

volume v

william s. peters, sr.

Now Available
www.innerchildpress.com

Inner Child Press News

The Book of krisar

Volume I

william s. peters, sr.

The Book of krisar

Volume II

william s. peters, sr.

Now Available
www.innerchildpress.com

The Year of the Poet XI ~ April 2024

The Book of krisar
Volume III

william s. peters, sr.

The Book of krisar
Volume IV

william s. peters, sr.

Now Available
www.innerchildpress.com

Inner Child Press News

Now Available
www.innerchildpress.com

The Year of the Poet XI ~ April 2024

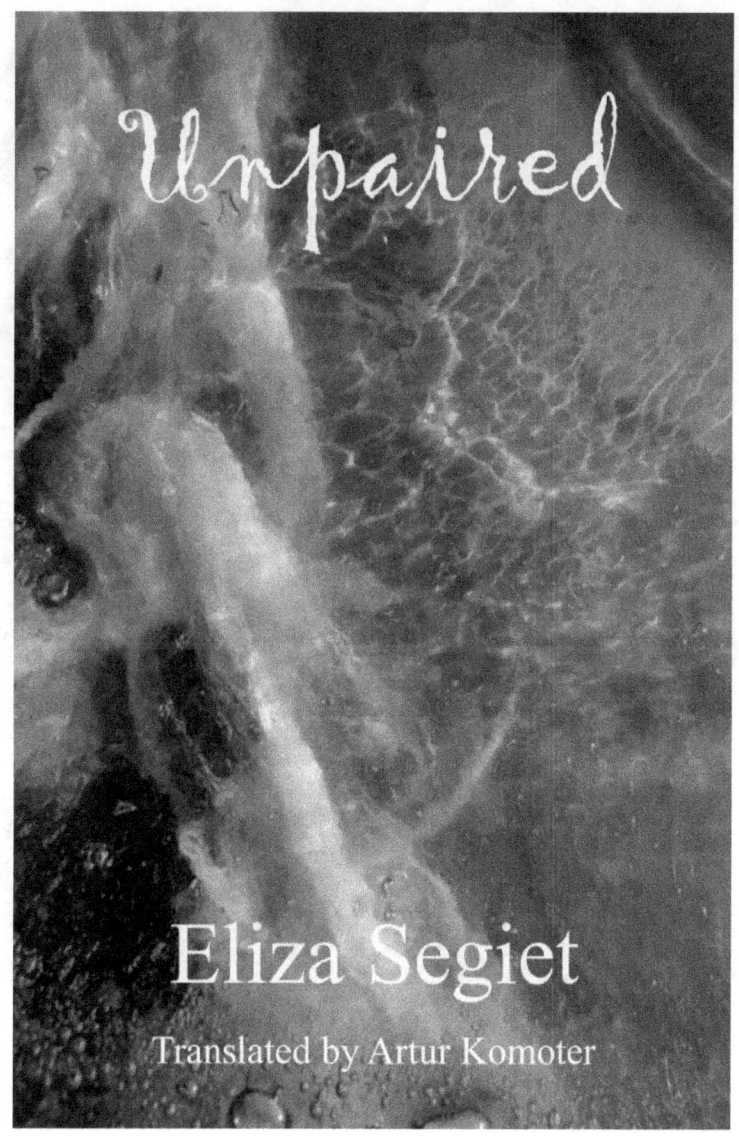

Private Issue
www.innerchildpress.com

Inner Child Press News

Canlarım
My Lifeblood

poetry in Turkish and English

hülya n. yılmaz

Now Available
www.innerchildpress.com

The Year of the Poet XI ~ April 2024

Now Available at
www.innerchildpress.com

Inner Child Press News

No Illusions
Through the Looking Glass

Jackie Davis Allen

Now Available at
www.innerchildpress.com

The Year of the Poet XI ~ April 2024

Now Available at
www.innerchildpress.com

Inner Child Press News

Now Available at
www.innerchildpress.com

The Year of the Poet XI ~ April 2024

HERENOW

FAHREDIN SHEHU

Now Available at
www.innerchildpress.com

Inner Child Press News

Now Available at
www.innerchildpress.com

The Year of the Poet XI ~ April 2024

Dark Side of the Moon

Jackie Davis Allen

Now Available at
www.innerchildpress.com

Now Available at
www.innerchildpress.com

The Year of the Poet XI ~ April 2024

Now Available at
www.innerchildpress.com

Inner Child Press News

Now Available at
www.innerchildpress.com

The Year of the Poet XI ~ April 2024

Breakfast for Butterflies

Faleeha Hassan

Now Available at
www.innerchildpress.com

Inner Child Press News

Now Available at
www.innerchildpress.com

The Year of the Poet XI ~ April 2024

Now Available at
www.innerchildpress.com

Inner Child Press News

Now Available at
www.innerchildpress.com

The Year of the Poet XI ~ April 2024

Inner Child Press News

Other Anthological works from

Inner Child Press International

www.innerchildpress.com

Inner Child Press Anthologies

Now Available
www.worldhealingworldpeacepoetry.com

Inner Child Press Anthologies

Now Available
www.worldhealingworldpeacepoetry.com

Inner Child Press Anthologies

Now Available
www.worldhealingworldpeacepoetry.com

Inner Child Press Anthologies

Now Available
www.innerchildpress.com

Inner Child Press Anthologies

Inner Child Press International
&
The Year of the Poet
present

Poetry
the best of 2020

Poets of the World

Now Available
www.innerchildpress.com

Inner Child Press Anthologies

Now Available
www.innerchildpress.com

Inner Child Press Anthologies

Now Available
www.innerchildpress.com

Inner Child Press Anthologies

Now Available
www.innerchildpress.com

Inner Child Press Anthologies

Now Available at
www.innerchildpress.com

Inner Child Press Anthologies

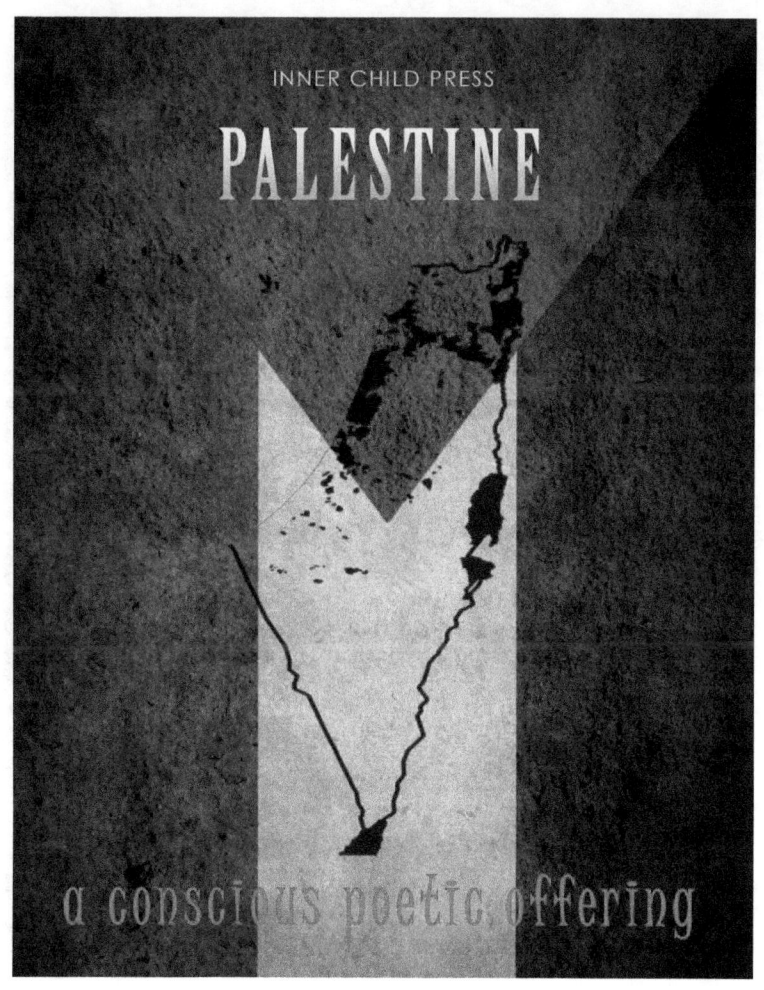

Now Available at
www.innerchildpress.com

Inner Child Press Anthologies

Now Available at
www.innerchildpress.com

Inner Child Press Anthologies

Now Available
www.worldhealingworldpeacepoetry.com

Inner Child Press Anthologies

Now Available
www.worldhealingworldpeacepoetry.com

Inner Child Press Anthologies

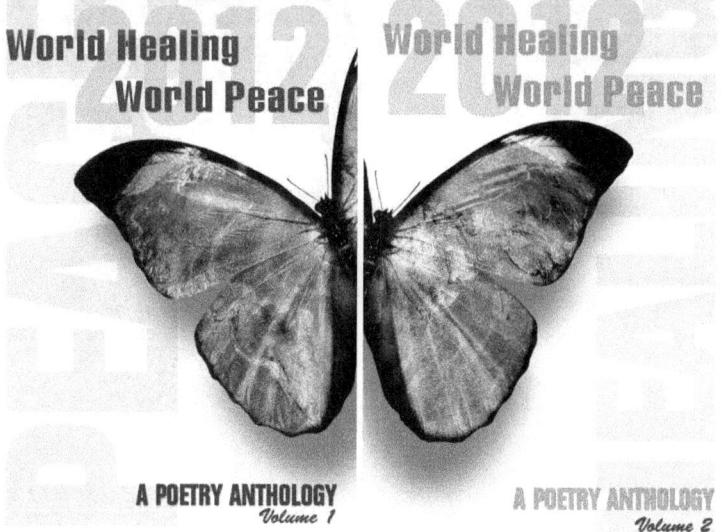

Now Available
www.worldhealingworldpeacepoetry.com

Inner Child Press Anthologies

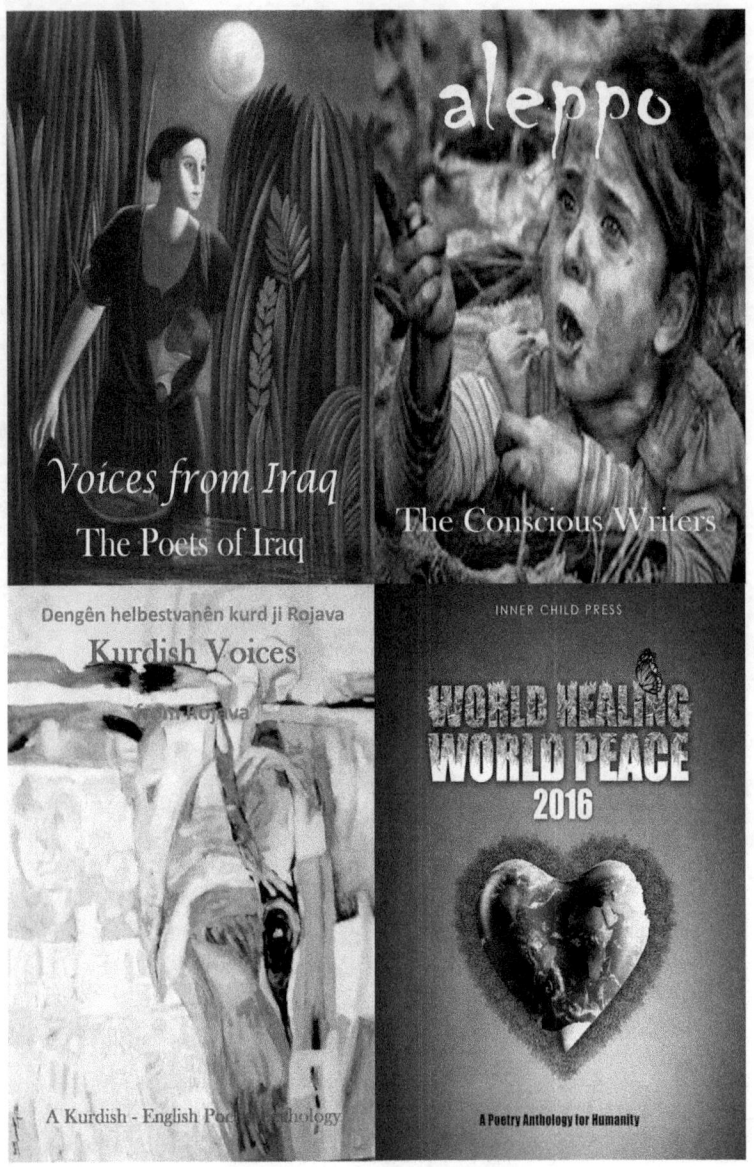

Now Available
www.innerchildpress.com/anthologies

Inner Child Press Anthologies

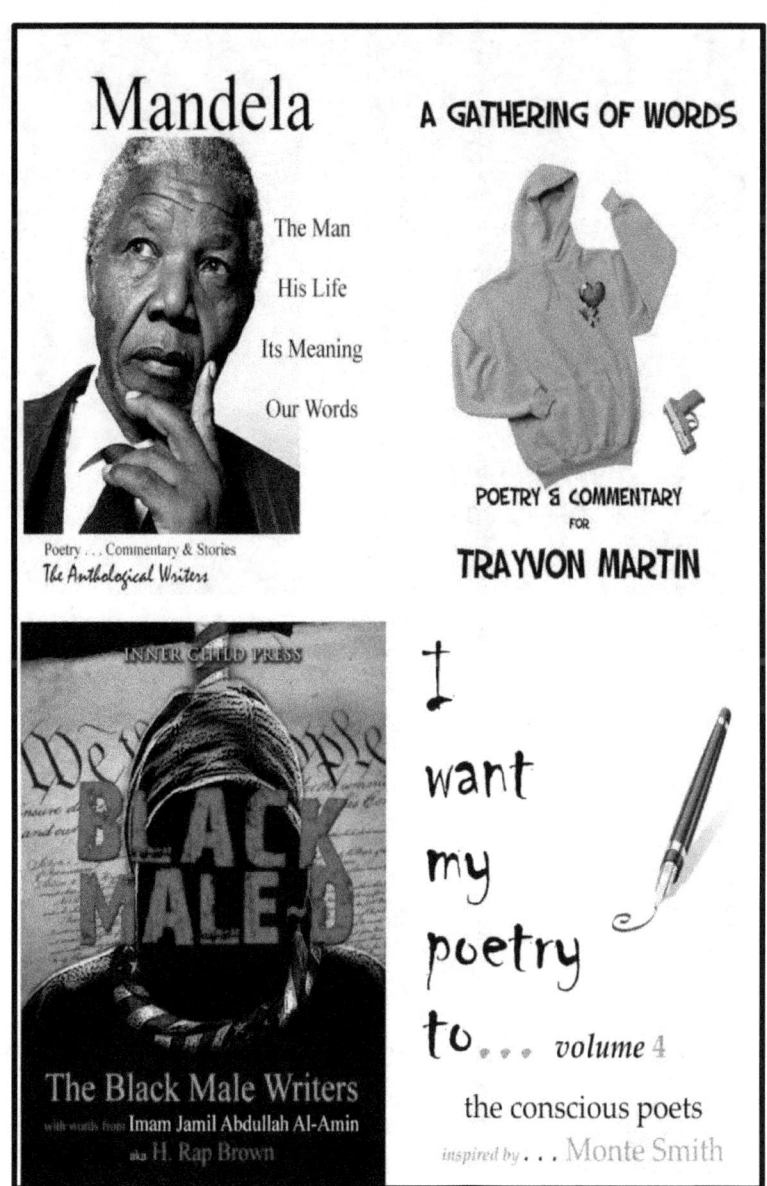

Now Available

www.innerchildpress.com/anthologies

Inner Child Press Anthologies

Now Available

www.innerchildpress.com/anthologies

Inner Child Press Anthologies

Now Available
www.innerchildpress.com/anthologies

Inner Child Press Anthologies

Now Available
www.innerchildpress.com/anthologies

Inner Child Press Anthologies

Now Available
www.innerchildpress.com/the-year-of-the-poet

Inner Child Press Anthologies

Now Available

www.innerchildpress.com/the-year-of-the-poet

Inner Child Press Anthologies

Now Available
www.innerchildpress.com/the-year-of-the-poet

Inner Child Press Anthologies

Now Available
www.innerchildpress.com/the-year-of-the-poet

Inner Child Press Anthologies

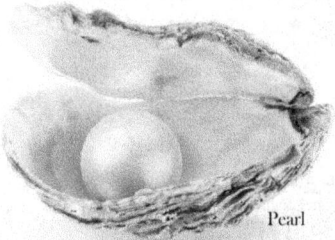

Now Available
www.innerchildpress.com/the-year-of-the-poet

Inner Child Press Anthologies

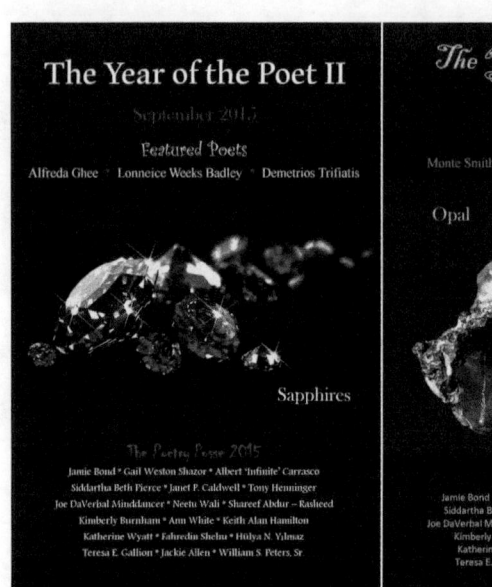

Now Available
www.innerchildpress.com/the-year-of-the-poet

Now Available
www.innerchildpress.com/the-year-of-the-poet

Inner Child Press Anthologies

Now Available
www.innerchildpress.com/the-year-of-the-poet

Inner Child Press Anthologies

Now Available
www.innerchildpress.com/the-year-of-the-poet

Inner Child Press Anthologies

Now Available
www.innerchildpress.com/the-year-of-the-poet

Inner Child Press Anthologies

Now Available
www.innerchildpress.com/the-year-of-the-poet

Inner Child Press Anthologies

The Year of the Poet IV
September 2017

Featured Poets
Martina Reisz Newberry
Ameer Nassir
Christine Fulco Neal
Robert Neal

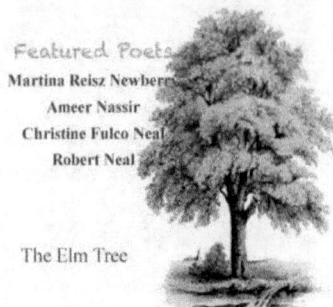

The Elm Tree

The Poetry Posse 2017

Gail Weston Shazor * Caroline Nazareno * Bismay Mohanty
Teresa E. Gallion * Anna Jakubczak Vel Ratty Adalan
Joe DaVerbal Minddancer * Shareef Abdur – Rasheed
Albert Carrasco * Kimberly Burnham * Elizabeth Castillo
Hülya N. Yılmaz * Faleeha Hassan * Jackie Davis Allen
Jen Walls * Nizar Sartawi * * William S. Peters, Sr.

The Year of the Poet IV
October 2017

Featured Poets
Ahmed Abu Saleem
Nedal Al-Qaeim
Sadeddin Shahin

The Black Walnut Tree

The Poetry Posse 2017

Gail Weston Shazor * Caroline Nazareno * Bismay Mohanty
Teresa E. Gallion * Anna Jakubczak Vel Ratty Adalan
Joe DaVerbal Minddancer * Shareef Abdur – Rasheed
Albert Carrasco * Kimberly Burnham * Elizabeth Castillo
Hülya N. Yılmaz * Faleeha Hassan * Jackie Davis Allen
Jen Walls * Nizar Sartawi * * William S. Peters, Sr.

The Year of the Poet IV
November 2017

Featured Poets
Kay Peters
Alfreda D. Ghee
Gabriella Garofalo
Rosemary Cappello

The Tree of Life

The Poetry Posse 2017

Gail Weston Shazor * Caroline Nazareno * Bismay Mohanty
Teresa E. Gallion * Anna Jakubczak Vel Ratty Adalan
Joe DaVerbal Minddancer * Shareef Abdur – Rasheed
Albert Carrasco * Kimberly Burnham * Elizabeth Castillo
Hülya N. Yılmaz * Faleeha Hassan * Jackie Davis Allen
Jen Walls * Nizar Sartawi * William S. Peters, Sr.

The Year of the Poet IV
December 2017

Featured Poets
Justice Clarke
Mariel M. Pabroa
Kiley Brown

The Fig Tree

The Poetry Posse 2017

Gail Weston Shazor * Caroline Nazareno * Bismay Mohanty
Teresa E. Gallion * Anna Jakubczak Vel Ratty Adalan
Joe DaVerbal Minddancer * Shareef Abdur – Rasheed
Albert Carrasco * Kimberly Burnham * Elizabeth Castillo
Hülya N. Yılmaz * Faleeha Hassan * Jackie Davis Allen
Jen Walls * Nizar Sartawi * William S. Peters, Sr.

Now Available
www.innerchildpress.com/the-year-of-the-poet

Inner Child Press Anthologies

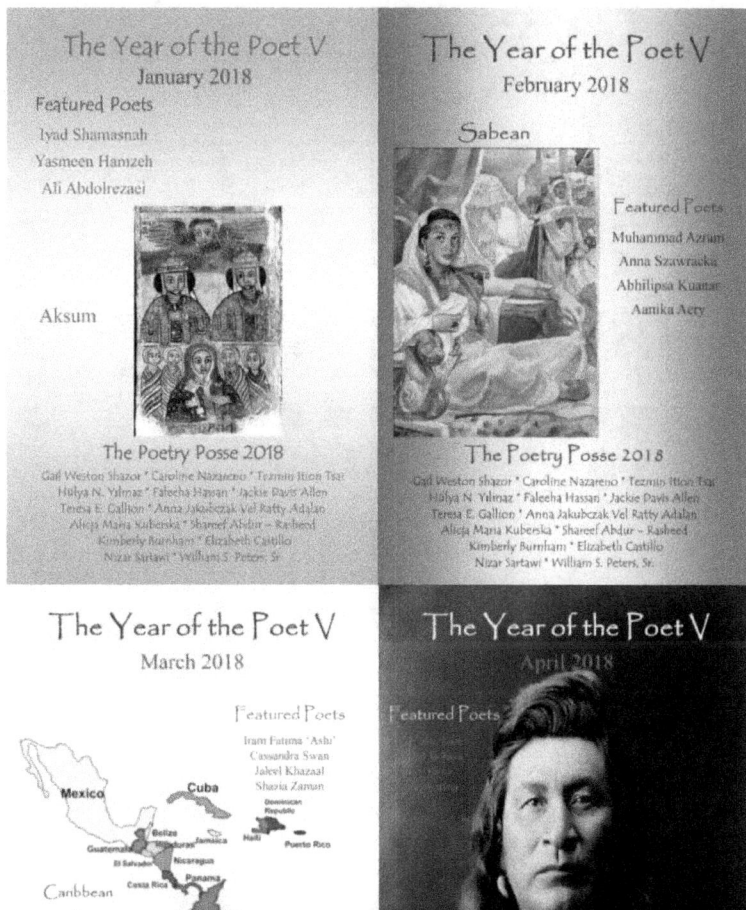

Now Available
www.innerchildpress.com/the-year-of-the-poet

Inner Child Press Anthologies

Now Available
www.innerchildpress.com/the-year-of-the-poet

Inner Child Press Anthologies

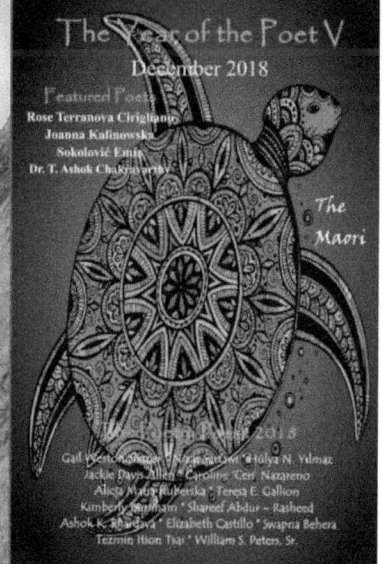

Now Available
www.innerchildpress.com/the-year-of-the-poet

Inner Child Press Anthologies

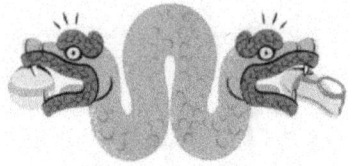

Now Available
www.innerchildpress.com/the-year-of-the-poet

Inner Child Press Anthologies

Now Available
www.innerchildpress.com/the-year-of-the-poet

Inner Child Press Anthologies

Now Available
www.innerchildpress.com/the-year-of-the-poet

Inner Child Press Anthologies

Now Available
www.innerchildpress.com/the-year-of-the-poet

Inner Child Press Anthologies

The Year of the Poet VII
May 2020

Featured Poets
Alok Kumar Ray * Eden S. Trinidad
Franco Barbato * Izabela Zubko

Ralph Bunche ~ 1950

The Year of Peace
Celebrating past Nobel Peace Prize Recipients

The Poetry Posse 2020
Gail Weston Shazor * Albert Carasico * Hülya N. Yılmaz
Jackie Davis Allen * Caroline Nazareno * Eliza Segiet
Alicja Maria Kuberska * Teresa E. Gallion * Joe Paire
Kimberly Burnham * Shareef Abdur – Rasheed
Ashok K. Bhargava * Elizabeth Castillo * Swapna Behera
Tezmin Ition Tsai * William S. Peters, Sr.

The Year of the Poet VII
June 2020

Featured Poets
Eftichia Kapardeli * Metin Cengiz
Hussein Habasch * Kosh K Mathew

Albert John Lutuli ~ 1960

The Year of Peace
Celebrating past Nobel Peace Prize Recipients

The Poetry Posse 2020
Gail Weston Shazor * Albert Carasico * Hülya N. Yılmaz
Jackie Davis Allen * Caroline Nazareno * Eliza Segiet
Alicja Maria Kuberska * Teresa E. Gallion * Joe Paire
Kimberly Burnham * Shareef Abdur – Rasheed
Ashok K. Bhargava * Elizabeth Castillo * Swapna Behera
Tezmin Ition Tsai * William S. Peters, Sr.

The Year of the Poet VII
July 2020

Featured Poets
Mykola Martyniuk * Orbindu Ganga
Roula Pollard * Karn Praktisha

Norman Ernest Borlaug ~ 1970

The Year of Peace
Celebrating past Nobel Peace Prize Recipients

The Poetry Posse 2020
Gail Weston Shazor * Albert Carasico * Hülya N. Yılmaz
Jackie Davis Allen * Caroline Nazareno * Eliza Segiet
Alicja Maria Kuberska * Teresa E. Gallion * Joe Paire
Kimberly Burnham * Shareef Abdur – Rasheed
Ashok K. Bhargava * Elizabeth Castillo * Swapna Behera
Tezmin Ition Tsai * William S. Peters, Sr.

The Year of the Poet VII
August 2020

Featured Poets
Dr Pragya Suman * Chinh Nguyen
Srinivas Vasudev * Ugwu Leonard Ifeanyi, Jr.

Adolfo Pérez Esquivel ~ 1980

The Year of Peace
Celebrating past Nobel Peace Prize Recipients

The Poetry Posse 2020
Gail Weston Shazor * Albert Carasico * Hülya N. Yılmaz
Jackie Davis Allen * Caroline Nazareno * Eliza Segiet
Alicja Maria Kuberska * Teresa E. Gallion * Joe Paire
Kimberly Burnham * Shareef Abdur – Rasheed
Ashok K. Bhargava * Elizabeth Castillo * Swapna Behera
Tezmin Ition Tsai * William S. Peters, Sr.

Now Available
www.innerchildpress.com/the-year-of-the-poet

Inner Child Press Anthologies

Now Available
www.innerchildpress.com/the-year-of-the-poet

Inner Child Press Anthologies

The Year of the Poet VIII
January 2021

Featured Global Poets
Andrew Scott * Debaprasanna Biswas
Shakil Kalam * Changming Yuan

Banksy's The Girl with the Pierced Eardrum

Poetry ... Ekphrasticly Speaking
The Poetry Posse 2020
Gail Weston Shazor * Albert Carasco * Hülya N. Yılmaz
Jackie Davis Allen * Caroline Nazareno * Eliza Segiet
Alicja Maria Kuberska * Teresa E. Gallion * Joe Paire
Kimberly Burnham * Shareef Abdur – Rasheed
Ashok K. Bhargava * Elizabeth Castillo * Swapna Behera
Tezmin Ition Tsai * William S. Peters, Sr.

The Year of the Poet VIII
February 2021

Featured Global Poets
T. Ramesh Babu * Ruchida Barman
Neptune Barman * Faleeha Hassan

Emory Douglas : 1968 Olympics mural

Poetry ... Ekphrasticly Speaking
The Poetry Posse 2021
Gail Weston Shazor * Albert Carasco * Hülya N. Yılmaz
Jackie Davis Allen * Caroline Nazareno * Eliza Segiet
Alicja Maria Kuberska * Teresa E. Gallion * Joe Paire
Kimberly Burnham * Shareef Abdur – Rasheed
Ashok K. Bhargava * Elizabeth Castillo * Swapna Behera
Tezmin Ition Tsai * William S. Peters, Sr.

The Year of the Poet VIII
March 2021

Featured Global Poets
Claudia Piccinno * Mohammed Jabr
Luzviminda Rivera * Nigar Arif

Tatyana Fazlalizadeh

Poetry ... Ekphrasticly Speaking
The Poetry Posse 2021
Gail Weston Shazor * Albert Carasco * Hülya N. Yılmaz
Jackie Davis Allen * Caroline Nazareno * Eliza Segiet
Alicja Maria Kuberska * Teresa E. Gallion * Joe Paire
Kimberly Burnham * Shareef Abdur – Rasheed
Ashok K. Bhargava * Elizabeth Castillo * Swapna Behera
Tezmin Ition Tsai * William S. Peters, Sr.

The Year of the Poet VIII
April 2021

Featured Global Poets
Katarzyna Brus- Sawczuk * Anwesha Paul
Rozalia Aleksandrova * Shahid Abbas

Pablo O'Higgins

Poetry ... Ekphrasticly Speaking
The Poetry Posse 2021
Gail Weston Shazor * Albert Carasco * Hülya N. Yılmaz
Jackie Davis Allen * Caroline Nazareno * Eliza Segiet
Alicja Maria Kuberska * Teresa E. Gallion * Joe Paire
Kimberly Burnham * Shareef Abdur – Rasheed
Ashok K. Bhargava * Elizabeth Castillo * Swapna Behera
Tezmin Ition Tsai * William S. Peters, Sr.

Now Available
www.innerchildpress.com/the-year-of-the-poet

Inner Child Press Anthologies

Now Available
www.innerchildpress.com/the-year-of-the-poet

Inner Child Press Anthologies

The Year of the Poet VIII
September 2021

Featured Global Poets
Monsif Beroual * Sandesh Ghimire
Sharmila Poudel * Pavol Janik

Heather Jansch

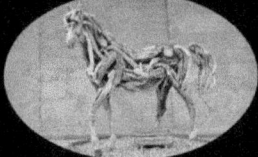

Poetry ... Ekphrasticly Speaking

The Poetry Posse 2021
Gail Weston Shazor * Albert Carasco * Hülya N. Yılmaz
Jackie Davis Allen * Caroline Nazareno * Eliza Segiet
Alicja Maria Kuberska * Teresa E. Gallion * Joe Paire
Kimberly Burnham * Shareef Abdur – Rasheed
Ashok K. Bhargava * Elizabeth Castillo * Swapna Behera
Tezmin Ition Tsai * William S. Peters, Sr.

The Year of the Poet VIII
October 2021

Featured Global Poets
C. E. Shy * Saswata Ganguly
Suranjit Gain * Hasiba Hilal

Dale Lamphere

Poetry ... Ekphrasticly Speaking

The Poetry Posse 2021
Gail Weston Shazor * Albert Carasco * Hülya N. Yılmaz
Jackie Davis Allen * Caroline Nazareno * Eliza Segiet
Alicja Maria Kuberska * Teresa E. Gallion * Joe Paire
Kimberly Burnham * Shareef Abdur – Rasheed
Ashok K. Bhargava * Elizabeth Castillo * Swapna Behera
Tezmin Ition Tsai * William S. Peters, Sr.

The Year of the Poet VIII
November 2021

Featured Global Poets
Errol D. Bean * Ibrahim Honjo
Tanja Ajtic * Rajashree Mohapatra

Andy Goldsworthy

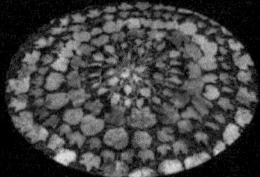

Poetry ... Ekphrasticly Speaking

The Poetry Posse 2021
Gail Weston Shazor * Albert Carasco * Hülya N. Yılmaz
Jackie Davis Allen * Caroline Nazareno * Eliza Segiet
Alicja Maria Kuberska * Teresa E. Gallion * Joe Paire
Kimberly Burnham * Shareef Abdur – Rasheed
Ashok K. Bhargava * Elizabeth Castillo * Swapna Behera
Tezmin Ition Tsai * William S. Peters, Sr.

The Year of the Poet VIII
December 2021

Featured Global Poets
Orbinda Ganga * Fadairo Tesleem
Anthony Arnold * Iyad Shamasnah

Fredric Edwin Church

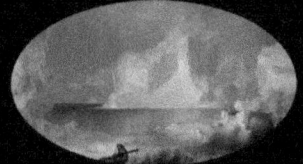

Poetry ... Ekphrasticly Speaking

The Poetry Posse 2021
Gail Weston Shazor * Albert Carasco * Hülya N. Yılmaz
Jackie Davis Allen * Caroline Nazareno * Eliza Segiet
Alicja Maria Kuberska * Teresa E. Gallion * Joe Paire
Kimberly Burnham * Shareef Abdur – Rasheed
Ashok K. Bhargava * Elizabeth Castillo * Swapna Behera
Tezmin Ition Tsai * William S. Peters, Sr.

Now Available

www.innerchildpress.com/the-year-of-the-poet

Inner Child Press Anthologies

The Year of the Poet IX
January 2022

Featured Global Poets
**Ratan Ghosh * Christine Neil-Wright
Andrew Scott * Ashok Kumar**

Climate Change : The Ice Cap

Poetry . . . Ekphrasticly Speaking

The Poetry Posse 2021

Gail Weston Shazor * Albert Carasco * Hülya N. Yılmaz
Jackie Davis Allen * Caroline Nazareno * Eliza Segiet
Alicja Maria Kuberska * Teresa E. Gallion * Joe Paire
Kimberly Burnham * Shareef Abdur – Rasheed
Ashok K. Bhargava * Elizabeth Castillo * Swapna Behera
Tezmin Ition Tsai * William S. Peters, Sr.

The Year of the Poet IX
February 2022

Featured Global Poets
**Roza Boyanova * Ramón de Jesús Núñez Duval
Mammad Ismayil * Tarana Turan Rahimli**

Climate Change and Mountains

Poetry . . . Ekphrasticly Speaking

The Poetry Posse 2021

Gail Weston Shazor * Albert Carasco * Hülya N. Yılmaz
Jackie Davis Allen * Caroline Nazareno * Eliza Segiet
Alicja Maria Kuberska * Teresa E. Gallion * Joe Paire
Kimberly Burnham * Shareef Abdur – Rasheed
Ashok K. Bhargava * Elizabeth Castillo * Swapna Behera
Tezmin Ition Tsai * William S. Peters, Sr.

The Year of the Poet IX
March 2022

Featured Global Poets
Dimitris P. Kraniotis * Marlene Pasini
Kennedy Ochieng * Swayam Prashant

Climate Change and Space Debris

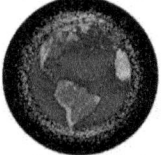

Poetry . . . Ekphrasticly Speaking

The Poetry Posse 2021

Gail Weston Shazor * Albert Carasco * Hülya N. Yılmaz
Jackie Davis Allen * Caroline Nazareno * Eliza Segiet
Alicja Maria Kuberska * Teresa E. Gallion * Joe Paire
Kimberly Burnham * Shareef Abdur – Rasheed
Ashok K. Bhargava * Elizabeth Castillo * Swapna Behera
Tezmin Ition Tsai * William S. Peters, Sr.

The Year of the Poet IX
April 2022

Featured Global Poets
**Alonzo Gross * Dr. Debaprasanna Biswas
Monsif Beroual * Carol Aronoff**

Climate Change and Oceans

Celebrating our 100th Edition

Poetry . . . Ekphrasticly Speaking

The Poetry Posse 2021

Gail Weston Shazor * Albert Carasco * Hülya N. Yılmaz
Jackie Davis Allen * Caroline Nazareno * Eliza Segiet
Alicja Maria Kuberska * Teresa E. Gallion * Joe Paire
Kimberly Burnham * Shareef Abdur – Rasheed
Ashok K. Bhargava * Elizabeth Castillo * Swapna Behera
Tezmin Ition Tsai * William S. Peters, Sr.

Now Available
www.innerchildpress.com/the-year-of-the-poet

Inner Child Press Anthologies

The Year of the Poet IX
May 2022

Featured Global Poets
Ndaba Sibanda * Smrutiranjan Mohanty
Ajanta Paul * Monalisa Dash Dwibedy

Climate Change and Birds

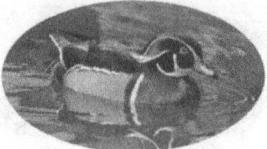

Poetry... Ekphrasticly Speaking

The Poetry Posse 2021

Gail Weston Shazor * Albert Carasco * Hülya N. Yılmaz
Jackie Davis Allen * Caroline Nazareno * Eliza Segiet
Alicja Maria Kuberska * Teresa E. Gallion * Joe Paire
Kimberly Burnham * Shareef Abdur – Rasheed
Ashok K. Bhargava * Elizabeth Castillo * Swapna Behera
Tezmin Ition Tsai * William S. Peters, Sr.

The Year of the Poet IX
June 2022

Featured Global Poets
Yuan Changming * Azeezat Okunlola
Tanja Ajtić * Philip Chijioke Abonyi

Climate Change and Trees

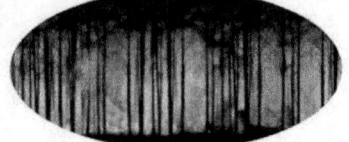

Poetry... Ekphrasticly Speaking

The Poetry Posse 2022

Gail Weston Shazor * Albert Carasco * Hülya N. Yılmaz
Jackie Davis Allen * Caroline Nazareno * Eliza Segiet
Alicja Maria Kuberska * Teresa E. Gallion * Joe Paire
Kimberly Burnham * Shareef Abdur – Rasheed
Ashok K. Bhargava * Elizabeth Castillo * Swapna Behera
Tezmin Ition Tsai * William S. Peters, Sr.

The Year of the Poet IX
July 2022

Featured Global Poets
Michelle Joan Barulich * Mili Das
Anna Ferriero * Ujjal Mandal

Climate Change and Animals

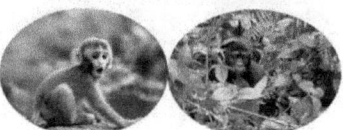

Poetry... Ekphrasticly Speaking

The Poetry Posse 2022

Gail Weston Shazor * Albert Carasco * Hülya N. Yılmaz
Jackie Davis Allen * Caroline Nazareno * Eliza Segiet
Alicja Maria Kuberska * Teresa E. Gallion * Joe Paire
Kimberly Burnham * Shareef Abdur – Rasheed
Ashok K. Bhargava * Elizabeth Castillo * Swapna Behera
Tezmin Ition Tsai * William S. Peters, Sr.

The Year of the Poet IX
August 2022

Featured Global Poets
Pankhuri Sinha * Abdulloh Abdumominov
Caroline Turunç * Tali Cohen Shabtai

Climate Change and Agriculture

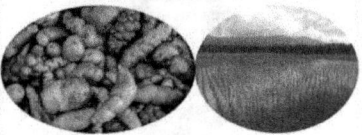

Poetry... Ekphrasticly Speaking

The Poetry Posse 2022

Gail Weston Shazor * Albert Carasco * Hülya N. Yılmaz
Jackie Davis Allen * Caroline Nazareno * Eliza Segiet
Alicja Maria Kuberska * Teresa E. Gallion * Joe Paire
Kimberly Burnham * Shareef Abdur – Rasheed
Ashok K. Bhargava * Elizabeth Castillo * Swapna Behera
Tezmin Ition Tsai * William S. Peters, Sr.

Now Available
www.innerchildpress.com/the-year-of-the-poet

Inner Child Press Anthologies

The Year of the Poet IX
September 2022

Featured Global Poets
Ngozi Olivia Osuoha * Biswajit Mishra
Sylwia K. Malinowska * Sajid Hussein

Climate Change and Wind and Weather Patterns

Poetry ... Ekphrasticly Speaking

The Poetry Posse 2022

Gail Weston Shazor * Albert Carasco * Hülya N. Yılmaz
Jackie Davis Allen * Caroline Nazareno * Eliza Segiet
Alicja Maria Kuberska * Teresa E. Gallion * Joe Paire
Kimberly Burnham * Shareef Abdur – Rasheed
Ashok K. Bhargava * Elizabeth Castillo * Swapna Behera
Tezmin Ition Tsai * William S. Peters, Sr.

The Year of the Poet IX
October 2022

Featured Global Poets
Andrew Kouroupos * Brenda Mohammed
Carthornia Kouroupos * Faleeha Hassan

Climate Change and Oil and Power

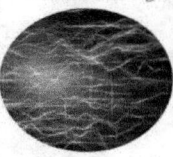 

Poetry ... Ekphrasticly Speaking

The Poetry Posse 2022

Gail Weston Shazor * Albert Carasco * Hülya N. Yılmaz
Jackie Davis Allen * Caroline Nazareno * Eliza Segiet
Alicja Maria Kuberska * Teresa E. Gallion * Joe Paire
Kimberly Burnham * Shareef Abdur – Rasheed
Ashok K. Bhargava * Elizabeth Castillo * Swapna Behera
Tezmin Ition Tsai * William S. Peters, Sr.

The Year of the Poet IX
November 2022

Featured Global Poets
Hema Ravi * Shafkat Aziz Hajam
Selma Kopic * Ibrahim Honjo

Climate Change : Time to Act

Poetry ... Ekphrasticly Speaking

The Poetry Posse 2022

Gail Weston Shazor * Albert Carasco * Hülya N. Yılmaz
Jackie Davis Allen * Caroline Nazareno * Eliza Segiet
Alicja Maria Kuberska * Teresa E. Gallion * Joe Paire
Kimberly Burnham * Shareef Abdur – Rasheed
Ashok K. Bhargava * Elizabeth Castillo * Swapna Behera
Tezmin Ition Tsai * William S. Peters, Sr.

The Year of the Poet IX
December 2022

Featured Global Poets
Elarbi Abdelfattah * Lorraine Cragg
Neha Bhandarkar * Robert Gibbons

Climate Change Bees, Butterflies and Insect Life

Poetry ... Ekphrasticly Speaking

The Poetry Posse 2022

Gail Weston Shazor * Albert Carasco * Hülya N. Yılmaz
Jackie Davis Allen * Caroline Nazareno * Eliza Segiet
Alicja Maria Kuberska * Teresa E. Gallion * Joe Paire
Kimberly Burnham * Shareef Abdur – Rasheed
Ashok K. Bhargava * Elizabeth Castillo * Swapna Behera
Tezmin Ition Tsai * William S. Peters, Sr.

Now Available
www.innerchildpress.com/the-year-of-the-poet

Inner Child Press Anthologies

Now Available

www.innerchildpress.com/the-year-of-the-poet

Inner Child Press Anthologies

Now Available
www.innerchildpress.com/the-year-of-the-poet

Inner Child Press Anthologies

The Year of the Poet X
September 2023

Featured Global Poets
Eftichia Karpadeli * Chinh Nguyen
Nigar Agalarova * Carmela Cueva

Children : Difference Makers

~ Easton LaChappelle ~
The Poetry Posse 2023

Gail Weston Shazor * Albert Carasco * Hülya N. Yılmaz
Jackie Davis Allen * Caroline Nazareno * Kimberly Burnham
Alicja Maria Kuberska * Teresa E. Gallion * Joe Paire
Michelle Joan Barulich * Shareef Abdur – Rasheed
Ashok K. Bhargava * Elizabeth Castillo * Swapna Behera
Tezmin Ition Tsai * Eliza Segiet * William S. Peters, Sr.

The Year of the Poet X
October 2023

Featured Global Poets
CSP Shrivastava * Huniie Parker
Noreen Snyder * Ramkrishna Paul

Children : Difference Makers

~ Malala Yousafzai ~
The Poetry Posse 2023

Gail Weston Shazor * Albert Carasco * Hülya N. Yılmaz
Jackie Davis Allen * Caroline Nazareno * Kimberly Burnham
Alicja Maria Kuberska * Teresa E. Gallion * Joe Paire
Michelle Joan Barulich * Shareef Abdur – Rasheed
Ashok K. Bhargava * Elizabeth Castillo * Swapna Behera
Tezmin Ition Tsai * Eliza Segiet * William S. Peters, Sr.

The Year of the Poet X
November 2023

Featured Global Poets
Ibrahim Honjo * Balachandran Nair
Xanthi Hondrou-Hil * Francesco Favetta

Children : Difference Makers

~ Jean-Michel Basquiat ~
The Poetry Posse 2023

Gail Weston Shazor * Albert Carasco * Hülya N. Yılmaz
Jackie Davis Allen * Caroline Nazareno * Kimberly Burnham
Alicja Maria Kuberska * Teresa E. Gallion * Joe Paire
Michelle Joan Barulich * Shareef Abdur – Rasheed
Ashok K. Bhargava * Elizabeth Castillo * Swapna Behera
Tezmin Ition Tsai * Eliza Segiet * William S. Peters, Sr.

The Year of the Poet X
December 2023

Featured Global Poets
Caroline Laurent Turunc * Neha Bhandarkar
Shafkat Aziz Hajam * Elarbi Abdelfattah

Children : Difference Makers

~ Melati and Isabel Wijsen ~
The Poetry Posse 2023

Gail Weston Shazor * Albert Carasco * Hülya N. Yılmaz
Jackie Davis Allen * Caroline Nazareno * Kimberly Burnham
Alicja Maria Kuberska * Teresa E. Gallion * Joe Paire
Michelle Joan Barulich * Shareef Abdur – Rasheed
Ashok K. Bhargava * Elizabeth Castillo * Swapna Behera
Tezmin Ition Tsai * Eliza Segiet * William S. Peters, Sr.

Now Available
www.innerchildpress.com/the-year-of-the-poet

and there is much, much more !

visit . . .

www.innerchildpress.com/anthologies-sales-special.php

Also check out our Authors and all the wonderful Books Available at :

www.innerchildpress.com/authors-pages

Now Available

www.worldhealingworldpeacepoetry.com

Now Available

www.worldhealingworldpeacepoetry.com

World Healing World Peace
2012, 2014, 2016, 2018, 2020, 2022

Now Available

www.worldhealingworldpeacepoetry.com

Inner Child Press International

'building bridges of cultural understanding'

Meet the Board of Directors

William S. Peters, Sr.
Chair Person
Founder
Inner Child Enterprises
Inner Child Press

Hülya N Yılmaz
Director
Editing Services
Co-Chair Person

Fahredin B. Shehu
Director
Cultural Affairs

Elizabeth E. Castillo
Director
Recording Secretary

De'Andre Hawthorne
Director
Performance Poetry

Gail Weston Shazor
Director
Anthologies

Kimberly Burnham
Director
Cultural Ambassador
Pacific Northwest
USA

Ashok K. Bhargava
Director
WINAwards

Deborah Smart
Director
Publicity
Marketing

www.innerchildpress.com

Inner Child Press International
'building bridges of cultural understanding'

Meet our Cultural Ambassadors

Fahredin Shehu
Director of Cultural

Faleeha Hassan
Iraq – USA

Elizabeth E. Castillo
Philippines

Antoinette Coleman
Chicago
Midwest USA

Ananda Nepali
Nepal – Tibet
Northern India

Kimberly Burnham
Pacific Northwest
USA

Alicja Kuberska
Poland
Eastern Europe

Swapna Behera
India
Southeast Asia

Kolade O. Freedom
Nigeria
West Africa

Monsif Beroual
Morocco
Northern Africa

Ashok K. Bhargava
Canada

Tzemin Ition Tsai
Republic of China
Greater China

Alicia M. Ramírez
Mexico
Central America

Christena AV Williams
Jamaica
Caribbean

Louise Hudon
Eastern Canada

Aziz Mountassir
Morocco
Northern Africa

Shareef Abdur-Rasheed
Southeastern USA

Laure Charazac
France
Western Europe

Mohammad Ikbal Harb
Lebanon
Middle East

Mohamed Abdel
Aziz Shmeis
Egypt
Middle East

Hillary Mainga
Kenya
Eastern Africa

Josephus R. Johnson
Liberia

Mennadi Farah
Algeria

www.innerchildpress.com

This Anthological Publication
is underwritten solely by

Inner Child Press International

Inner Child Press is a Publishing Company Founded and Operated by Writers. Our personal publishing experiences provides us an intimate understanding of the sometimes daunting challenges Writers, New and Seasoned may face in the Business of Publishing and Marketing their Creative "Written Work".

For more Information

Inner Child Press International

www.innerchildpress.com

'building bridges of cultural understanding'
202 Wiltree Court, State College, Pennsylvania 16801

www.innerchildpress.com

~ fini ~

www.ingramcontent.com/pod-product-compliance
Lightning Source LLC
LaVergne TN
LVHW051043080426
835508LV00019B/1678